Fascism

Concepts in Social Thought

Series Editor: Frank Parkin

Published Titles

Concepts in Social Thought

Fascism

Mark Neocleous

University of Minnesota Press
Minneapolis

First published by Open University Press, 1997

Published simultaneously in the United States 1997
by the University of Minnesota Press
111 Third Avenue South, Suite 290
Minneapolis, MN 55401-2520

Printed in Great Britain

Library of Congress Cataloging-in-Publication Data
Neocleous, Mark, 1964–
    Fascism / Mark Neocleous
       p. cm. — (concepts in social thought)
    Includes bibliographical references and index.
    ISBN 0-8166-3039-9 (hardcover)   ISBN 0-8166-3040-2 (pbk.)
    1. Fascism I. Title. II. Series.
[JC481.N343   1997]
320.53′3—dc21   96-48811
                                                  CIP

The University of Minnesota is an
equal-opportunity educator and employer.

For Rachel and Helen de Beer

Contents

Acknowledgements

I thank: Peter Osborne once again for his careful scrutiny of the manuscript; Geoff Kay for his encouragement; Stuart Elden for his thoughtful comments; David Stevens for his assistance and support; those colleagues at Brunel University who endured some of these arguments on a ridiculously hot day in June 1995; and Rachel and Helen de Beer – to whom the book is dedicated – for being a constant reminder of the importance of the struggle against fascism and the conditions which give rise to it.

Preface

Fascism, one historian tells us, 'began in 1922–23 with the emergence of the Italian fascist party . . . came of age in the 1930s when "fascist" parties sprang up throughout Europe . . . [and] ended in 1945 with the defeat and death of the two dictators'.[1] This approach to fascism.has a remarkably convenient historical and conceptual simplicity, encouraging us to restrict our research to the period 1922–45 and inviting us to study the institutions and processes of fascist rule rather than fascist ideas and movements more generally. All the problems involved in identifying any kind of fascist minimum are overcome in an instant. Whatever 'precursors' of fascism there were before 1922, especially of an intellectual kind, are treated as largely parochial, and any difficulties in specifying the nature of fascism, its ideological essence and its continued existence, are side-tracked by ever more detailed accounts of the minutiae of the Italian or German regimes.

In particular, this approach underestimates the extent to which certain tendencies before 1922, with their origins in the nineteenth century and the intellectual milieu at its *fin de siècle*, formed the foundation for the development of fascism, and ignores the fact that this development was rooted in a particular set of *philosophical* debates rather than in a coherently organized political party or movement. The arguments in this book challenge this approach in two broad ways. In the first place, Europe's path to fascism in the sphere of philosophy (to paraphrase Georg Lukács) is central to my concern.[2] Far from being a parenthesis in European history, fascism is a product of philosophico-political struggles within European intellectual, cultural and political history, and, I shall argue, is in turn constitutive of that history. In the second place, I shall point to the fact that, far from being some kind of political aberration arising from the inability of small but active groups of people to grasp the essentials of 'civilized' bourgeois life, fascism is in fact a problem of the 'normal' organization of our lived relations.[3]

This book, then, will not be concerned with identifying as 'fascist' this or that particular movement, party, organization or regime; that is a task best left to political scientists and their instruments of comparison or contrast (whichever is currently in vogue). Neither is this book concerned with making yet another contribution to the increasingly voluminous historical literature on fascist states, near-fascist states, pre-fascist states, quasi-fascist states, and so on.[4] Anyone who reads any of this literature soon realizes that the years of fascism scholarship have to some extent been a debate concerning the very term 'fascism'. Indeed, fascism's tendency to denounce rational argument and glorify the non-rational – to pile up contradiction after contradiction – has meant that many commentators have given up trying to identify any conceptual core whatsoever, that is, they have given up trying to peer behind the veil of fascist appearance in order to identify a fascist essence. In extreme cases they have suggested that we give up talking about fascism completely, other than as a reference to something Italians experienced between the wars. In other words fascism, for them, is either empty of real meaning or only means something in the context of a short period in Italian history.

'Full of emotion and empty of real meaning, the word fascism is one of most abused and abusive in our political vocabulary', Gilbert Allardyce tells us.[5] Yet it is surely because the word is so full of emotion that it is not empty of meaning. The reasons why it is full of emotion are clear: anyone with any concern for human dignity can see the destructive effects of the fascist denigration of human life only as an affront to humanity. This gives 'fascism' some kind of meaning, albeit a deeply ambiguous one. Yet it also has meaning because we know that fascism touches on fundamental questions about the nature of the society we currently live in and the destructive potential it contains. Because the problem of fascism is a problem of our society and the nature of the social relations which shape our lives, any argument about fascism is simultaneously an argument about these relations. Any argument about fascism therefore necessarily involves a confrontation with the nature of modernity and, concomitantly, a confrontation with the nature of capitalism and democracy.[6] Seeing fascism as a historical phenomenon that ended in 1945 or thereabouts thus encourages a dangerous forgetting: failing to see that fascism is a feature of modernity, it fails to see that fascism has not died. Perhaps the reason why there is so much literature on fascism is less that it is fascinating (as Susan Sontag is nevertheless right to suggest)[7] and more that those who choose to write about fascism know that they are dealing with the destructive potential of modernity, even if they naively insist that this potential is now a thing of the past.

Fascism is first and foremost an ideology generated by modern industrial capitalism. As a system it is the negative potential – that is, the potential for human destruction – implicit in the nature of modernity and capitalism, and which confronts head-on the positive potential for human emancipation. The crux of this confrontation, the fulcrum around which this battle for the realization of the opposed potentialities of modernity takes place, is the politics of mass society. The argument in this book is that fascism is a politics implicit in modern capitalism, involving mass mobilization for nationalist and counter-revolutionary aims, militarized activism and a drive for an elitist, authoritarian and repressive state apparatus, articulated through a nebulous vitalist philosophy of nature and the will.

My argument focuses on three concepts central to fascism: war, nature and nation. Obliterating history from all political and social questions, fascism fills the vacuum left with a sanctification of nature and thus that which it takes to be natural: war and the nation. These concepts are intimately bound into the key aspect of fascism: that it is a counter-revolutionary phenomenon engaged in the prevention of communism, but which seeks none the less to provide an alternative revolutionary impetus to the social forces of mass society by mobilizing them through an aggressive nationalism and by appropriating and radicalizing central features of modernity for reactionary political goals ('revolution against the revolution'). The reading of fascism in the chapters which follow is that it is a form of reactionary modernism: responding to the alienation and exploitation of modern society but unwilling to lay down any serious challenge to the structure of private property central to modern capitalism, fascism can only set its compass by the light of reaction, a mythic past to be recaptured within the radically altered conditions of modernity. This politics of reaction constitutes the ideological basis of a revolution from the right in which war, nature and the nation become the central terms.

1
Perpetual War and the Destruction of Reason

'The year 1789 is hereby eradicated from history', said Goebbels, speaking of the Nazi seizure of power in 1933.[1] He was indeed expressing part of the truth: fascism emerged first and foremost as a reaction to the Enlightenment in general and the values propounded in the French revolution in particular – Mussolini repeatedly insisted that fascism was against everything that the French revolution was for. In one sense fascism can be understood as a movement to ensure that the Enlightenment project remains unfinished, indeed destroyed, for it began life as a philosophical controversy with the rationalism and idealism of the nineteenth century and the Enlightenment's core political projects of liberalism and Marxism; at the heart of its arguments lies an essentially anti-materialist misology. In fact, the controversy was not so much with rationalism and materialism, but with *mechanistic* versions of them, or what was often regarded as positivism. Crucial to this controversy were intellectual developments in the final decade of the nineteenth and first decade of the twentieth centuries. The 1890s have been described as the revolt against positivism, and it is this revolt rather than a straightforward anti-Enlightenment stance that was central to the emergence of fascism.[2] The concern in this chapter is, first, to outline the politics of this revolt (rather than simply identify it as a revolt), before exploring how the central categories with which Enlightenment discourse are replaced give rise to the glorification of war.

The politics of the revolt against positivism

A theory is rationalist when it invokes autonomous reason as the basis for human practice; institutions and processes of society are to be justified on the basis of reason. It assumes the rationality of the human subject (at least potentially so) and thus the possibility of a rational social order. For the liberal, the property relations of bourgeois society are essentially rational in that there can be no better system of production; the remaining questions concern the particular form of the political institutions of such a society and the extent of its distribution of socio-economic power and wealth. A rational economic system is held in place by the increasing rationalization of law and state power. Ultimately progress on the basis of reason is to be the corner-stone of social change. Marxism distances itself from liberal rationalism on the grounds that the latter merely serves to idealize bourgeois society. For Marxism, in contrast, reason is the basis for a *critical* theory of society, one which points not to the rational present but to a rational future, to be forged out of the irrationality of the present. Against the privatization of reason in liberal rationalism, Marxism posits collective emancipation by a class which, as the universal class, is committed to a truly rational society. Yet, despite these crucial differences between Marxism and liberalism, fascism treats them as the two sides of the same rationalist coin. Likewise, fascism re ;ards Marxism and liberalism as the two sides of materialism. All those who went on to become significant fascist intellectuals established themselves as key thinkers in opposition to materialism.

The 'fascicization' of social and political thought in the late nineteenth century, despite being never fully coherent and having a diverse range of roots, began with the revolt against positivism.[3] Disregarding momentarily the political intentions of the writers central to this revolt, its diverse roots challenged the central presuppositions of Western philosophy. Friedrich Nietzsche's philosophical revolt against reason and the herd mentality attacked the levelling process of the Enlightenment, proposing instead a 'new Enlightenment' which would be a 'transvaluation of all values', rooted in a certain conception of human *instinct* rather than reason. Instead of the Enlightenment demand that we use our reason as the basis for a moral order, encapsulated in the Kantian insistence that we act according to the categorical imperative,

Nietzsche insists that every sound morality is governed not by critical reason but by 'sound instinct', which is rooted in the entirely *natural* will: 'where I found a living creature, there I found a will to power'.[4] It is in expressing this will that 'real life' is to be found. This jargon of authenticity identifies the irrational will as the real determining force behind great civilization and the key determinant of politics and society.

In philosophical terms, Nietzsche's work encouraged others to shift away from rationalism and positivism. Henri Bergson's vitalist critique of Western philosophy, for example, replaces reason and intellect with intuition and the *élan vital*. Conceiving his work as a contribution to both philosophy and the science of matter, Bergson substitutes a nebulous 'life-philosophy' for the search for a theory of consciousness, and a principle of energy for the principles of mechanics found in the natural sciences. For Bergson, consciousness stretches beyond the limits of intelligence and reason. Distinguishing between a superficial psychic life and a life in the depths of consciousness, Bergson holds that whereas the standard scientific method is applicable for the former, for the latter a different method is required, for here one is exploring 'the deep-seated self'. To understand in what way consciousness goes beyond intelligence and reason one has to look inward, so to speak. Natural science and logic are the appropriate methods for the measurement and thus the understanding of space, but can never hope to grasp time as lived experience – duration. To understand this, introspection – understood as a consideration of one's own consciousness – is necessary. To grasp time as lived experience, *intuition* is required. Given this, Bergson is left with the individual will and its vital life force, and intuition as the real means for 'understanding' it. This not only transforms central philosophical issues into questions of psychology, but also privileges intuition and instinct, central as they are to the *élan vital*. And, in arguing that the way to be free is to 'grasp' ourselves, Bergson is left to argue that the only way to do this is through action. The rationalist enterprise of knowledge as the basis for action, in order that change might be thought through before being carried out, is replaced by action as the basis of self-understanding (intuition) and thus creative evolution.[5]

The arguments of Nietzsche and Bergson, combined with new work in physics (the gradual emergence of the theory of relativity), the development of psychoanalysis and its stress on unconscious motivation, and the increasing predominance in social and political thought of social Darwinism and its focus on struggle as the basis for survival, had a dramatic effect on political culture of the period. While the revolt against traditional philosophical questions instigated by writers such as Nietzsche and Bergson has long been identified as important to the rise of fascism, it is in fact the *politics* of this revolt that is crucial. The fact that this occurred in the late nineteenth century and not before is significant. For while fascism emerged as a response to the Enlightenment, anti-Enlightenment philosophy existed prior to the *fin de siècle* and included a long tradition of reactionary thinkers such as Burke, Carlyle and de Maistre. But this tradition could not be described as fascist. What made the difference was partly what has been described as a growing culture of despair – a feeling that decadence and degeneration had become so prevalent that civilization itself was under threat[6] – and, more importantly, the political baptism of the European working class. It is in the historic conjunction of anti-materialist misology and the growth of working-class politics that the roots of fascism lie, for fascism was a reaction to the communist and socialist forces which sought to mobilize the working class against private property and for a project of human emancipation. As ruling classes across Europe sought to cut off the possibility of communism by incorporating the working class into the existing social and political structures, and liberalism and conservatism began appropriating the language of democracy as part of this politics of containment, fascism sought to *mobilize* the masses, but for a very different political project – of radical reaction. That is, fascism continues the tradition of reactionary thought but in a radically new way – by mobilizing the masses in an anti-communist and anti-socialist project. In doing so it built on the revolt against positivism by appropriating its key themes and politicizing them explicitly. Here it built on crowd psychology, elitist theory and a certain kind of revision of Marxism.

In a series of texts in the 1890s on the psychology of mass behaviour, Gustave Le Bon outlined the 'laws' governing collective behaviour.[7] Collective action, for Le Bon, reveals that otherwise rational individuals engage in irrational behaviour when they are under the influence of the crowd. Collective behaviour is the behaviour of the irrational, the merely instinctive, even barbaric, in contrast to the rational behaviour of civilized minds. Despite his claim that his argument is as much about 'crowds' such as juries and parliamentary groups, Le Bon consistently identifies the 'crowd' with the working class and the modern socialist movement. Socialism is doomed to failure, Le Bon tells us, because it assumes that the crowd can be won over with rational arguments, whereas the crowd is in fact essentially primitive, even barbarian, and thus rooted in instinct and hostile to reason. Le Bon's conception of the essentially primitive nature of the crowd and its hostility to reason itself turns into a mass psychology hostile to reason.[8] The lesson taught by Le Bon, and heeded by fascism, is that this has *political* consequences for anyone who wishes to mobilize mass forces. It means that the crowd thinks in images and through sentimental slogans. It also means that the crowd has to be led by a strong-willed and determined leader. The leadership of any mass movement has to tap into its irrational core, utilize the irrational force and motivation of the crowd in order to make its movement successful:

> Given to exaggeration in its feelings, a crowd is only impressed by excessive sentiments. An orator wishing to move a crowd must make an abusive use of violent affirmations. To exaggerate, to affirm, to resort to repetitions, and never to attempt to prove anything by reasoning are methods of argument well known to speakers at public meetings.

Philosophy is useless here; because the crowd 'must have their illusions at all costs', whoever can supply them with illusions becomes their master. And it means, moreover, that the crowd has to be controlled, if necessary by an authoritarian power, not just in the service of social and political order, but because this is what the crowd wants: suffering from the 'sentiment of servitude', the crowd is always ready to 'bow down servilely before a strong authority'.[9]

This combination of mass psychology and apology for authoritarian rule was complemented by the newly emerging political sociology of elitism which, like crowd psychology, dressed up an attack on socialism as an explanation of elite–mass relations. In the early years of the twentieth century the work of Gaetano Mosca, Robert Michels and Vilfredo Pareto identified the circulation of elites (a term which only came into widespread use from the 1890s) as a permanent feature of social and political life. Michels, who started life as a Marxist and became a fascist, tested this theory on the German Social Democratic Party (SPD) which, as the largest socialist party in Europe and therefore committed to the democratic diffusion of power, offered the least favourable test case for the theory. Michels found that it too verified the 'iron law of oligarchy', that is, that elites were a necessary and natural form for organizations to take. Treating societies as large-scale organizations this means that societies too are always elitist; history is merely the graveyard of elites. To think otherwise, to believe that the increasing democratization of society can facilitate an increasing number of people in the governing of society, is to delude oneself.[10] Consciously echoing the first lines of *The Communist Manifesto*, Pareto claims that history is the history of struggle between elites. This approach to politics also has an irrationalist twist, in that one reason why elites exist is that the mass needs them to. Distinguishing between logical and non-logical (or rational and non-rational) behaviour, Pareto suggests that most people's behaviour is based on illusions regarding their motives. Because 'very frequently, individuals and groups are unaware of the forces prompting their behaviour' such actions are, in principle at least, incapable of being treated rationally. Humans are essentially non-rational creatures, subject not to the forces of reason but to instinct, sentiment, intuition and will.[11]

Now, whether the elitism of these writers explains their attachment to fascism (in the case of Michels and Pareto) when it came into power is less relevant than their explicitly political contribution to the intellectual and cultural revolution which paved the way for fascism. For the elitists, like Le Bon, were engaging in a conscious attack on socialism, Marxism and democracy in a language gleaned from the revolt against positivism and combined with political concepts diametrically opposed to those of revolutionary socialism but with similar connotations. This revolt generated the concepts which were to become central to fascism: elite, authority, instinct, vital forces, will to power, nature. That this occurred in the context of the political baptism of the working class is crucial, for some influential Marxists 'revised' Marx through the adoption of these concepts. The most obvious example is Mussolini, but it is worth considering first the trajectory of other influential thinkers. In France – regarded by some as the real birthplace of fascism[12] – this included Georges Sorel and Henrik de Man.

In his early career Georges Sorel believed that Marxism was 'the greatest innovation in philosophy' and 'an exact, absolute science of economic relationships', and he committed himself to its project in the language of Hegelian Marxism: 'that which is rational . . . ought to become real'. By the time he had made his own revision of Marx, however, he had come to regard his earlier work as 'full of rationalist prejudices'.[13] The rise of parliamentary democracy and the inclusion of the working class in society made a revision of Marx necessary. So when Eduard Bernstein's 'revision' of Marx gained widespread public attention in 1899, Sorel welcomed it. However, Bernstein's arguments led to political reformism – the ultimate aim of socialism, for Bernstein, was the gradual reform of capitalism through industrial democracy and an agreement on the funda- mental principles of political liberalism. Sorel, as a committed 'revolutionary', refused to have Marxism reduced to a political party focusing on electioneering and piecemeal reforms. Marxism was to be revised, but not in order to advance along the parlia- mentary road to 'bidets for everyone'; it had to remain 'unalterably committed to the idea of total revolution'.[14]

Sorel's alternative stresses class struggle, but his rejection of economic determinism means that the origin of struggle has to come from elsewhere. On the one hand it is to be rooted in the *ethics* of socialism. Economic factors are obviously important, as Marxism taught, but to regard these as the *determining* factor in historical change, in the manner of vulgar materialism, is misguided and inconsistent with Marx's own teaching. For Marxism is as much an ethical doctrine as an economic one. The very language Marx used in his critique of political economy – oppression, exploitation, misery – shows that Marx himself thought beyond mere economic forces. On the other hand, Sorel, having breathed the air of the new intellectual climate, argues that what motivates collective action is often a set of unconscious and non-rational motivations. The revision of Marx therefore needs a *psychology* of historical ma- terialism.[15]

What is this psychology to consist of? For Sorel, Marx employs 'social myth'. Treading a fine line between Blanquism and utopianism, Marx understands how collective action comes about through a combination of a vision of the future and a proper understanding of the present. Marx's *Capital* is, of course, a critique of political economy. But, 'we must not take the text literally. We are in the realm of . . . *social myth*'.[16] Social myths act as mobilizing forces, resting on both the moral injunctions underlying them and on imagined futures. Their purpose is to foster action and engage the will. They may be able to be expressed in a scientific fashion, but their essential feature is that they tap into the collective and irrational forces which bind collective agents. 'The movements of the revolted masses must be represented in such a way that the soul of the revolutionaries may receive a deep and lasting impression'. For this to be achieved,

> use must be made of a *body of images* which, by *intuition* alone, and before any considered analyses are made, is capable of evoking as an undivided whole the *mass of sentiments* which corresponds to the different manifestations of the war undertaken by Socialism.[17]

The revolutionary syndicalist movement had solved the problem, Sorel believed, with the myth of the general strike. Such a social myth cannot be understood in a scientific (that is, 'mechanistic') way, and Sorel castigates those who claimed that the general strike is not practically possible by insisting that in order to mobilize collective action one had to have some vision of an alternative future which avoided the utopian socialist error of planning the future, but which appealed to a collective instinct for a future transformation. Thus Sorel posits the social myth as a mobilizing force rooted in an image of the future while simultaneously castigating the utopians for planning the future in a rationalist fashion. The social myth of the general strike is designed to tap into the collective irrational forces that exist, to appeal not to reason but to sentiment, to mobilize not on the basis of knowledge but on the basis of action. And, crucially, what is needed to understand it is not the application of science or the methods of science, but *intuition*, the ' "global knowledge" of Bergson's philosophy': 'we thus obtain that intuition of Socialism which language cannot give us with perfect clearness – and we obtain it as a whole, perceived instantaneously'.[18] Here Bergson is used to fill the gaps necessarily left in any theory of myth. As Gramsci recognized, in Sorel's work there is

> a conflict of two necessities: that of the myth, and that of the critique of the myth – in that 'every pre-established plan is utopian and reactionary'. The outcome [is] left to the intervention of the irrational, to chance (in the Bergsonian sense of '*élan vital*') or to 'spontaneity'.[19]

Sorel's revisionism divests Marxism of mechanistic scientism but retains and highlights the apocalyptic moment, concentrated in the revolutionary class struggle, which explodes at key historical conjunctures. The attempt to reconstitute Marxism as a real mobilizing force turns Marx's critique of political economy into an ethics, Marx's materialism into vitalism, and Marx's analysis of class struggle into collective will expressed via irrational myths. Class action is separated from any social purpose and becomes an end in itself. A similar task was performed by Henrik de Man. Like Sorel, de Man revises Marx by raising the question of motivation. His key work, *Zur Psychologie des Sozialismus* (1926) was translated into French as *Au-delà du marxisme*: understanding the *psychology* of socialism constituted the move *beyond* Marxism. By the time he came to write this book, de Man was sure of two things: first, that Marx's materialism was one of the main reasons for the collapse of socialism; and second, that the First World War had shown that socialism was not a revolutionary force, because it was not a belief for which people were willing to die.

The problem with Marxism, for de Man, is that it remains steeped in the nineteenth century – determinist, mechanistic, rationalist and economistic.[20] Marxism insists that what determines social activity is knowledge, and knowledge of a particular kind. Being economistic, Marxism has to insist that it is knowledge of relations of production which determines social action. This 'theory of motives' assumes that social action by the masses is determined by their knowledge of their class interests; the whole approach is thus rationalist and economistic. De Man poses two related problems at this. First, the fact that large numbers of important socialist writers and activists have been bourgeois proves that socialism did not simply emerge from class interests. Instead it is a product of an *ethics*, a distinctive socialist ethics not limited to a particular class. Second, workers often become socialist not through any rational motive but through *affective* phenomena, a mass affect, which gives rise to social action. 'Not until we have made an exhaustive study of the worker's *emotive* reaction to his social environment, can we understand the part played by socialist theories'. Class war is born not out of class consciousness, but from 'the *feeling* of class resentment'.[21] Rather than seek the motives for mass action in reasoned class consciousness, our attention should be directed to the feelings and affects that give rise to it. Socialism, then, is a product not of class struggle, but of a will to struggle on the grounds of certain ethical values. This turns socialist 'theory' into a *passion* rather than a reasoned argument, a *faith* rather than a science, and the struggle for socialism into the struggle for an *image* of the future which one *believes* in rather than the struggle for a rational society. In support of his argument, de Man invokes the science of psychology (at least as he understands it): against Marx's account of class interest de Man suggests that

> evaluation [of interest] and need [of fulfilment] both presuppose an emotional reaction that takes place as such in the unconscious . . . Shifts in the collective unconscious furnish the lowest common denominator for the formula that expresses the relations of mutual dependence on the pattern of development of interests and ideas.[22]

As Zeev Sternhell points out, de Man was well aware that he was invoking the Sorelian notion of myth. Their joint revision of Marxism replaces Marxism's materialism and determinism with *voluntarism* and *vitalism*.[23] In presenting the question of socialism as the question of ethical values and the psychology of the workers feeling these values, de Man turns the problem of socialism into the psychology of instinct, culminating in the claim that the most important feature of socialism is the struggle itself. As with Bernstein's social democratic revisionism – in which the goal is nothing but the movement everything – the revision of Marx peddled by Sorel and de Man points to the movement too, but only the movement as satisfying the socialist 'urge' in and of itself. In other words, action becomes the basis for the satisfaction of the unconscious urge towards ethical values.

This revision of Marxism helped pave the intellectual way for fascism. Georges Valois openly hailed Sorel as 'the intellectual father of fascism', and Mussolini claimed that 'what I am, I owe to Sorel' (to which Sorel replied by describing Mussolini as a man of greater reach than all the statesmen of the day). And in an exchange of letters in 1930 Mussolini describes de Man's criticisms of Marxism as 'definitive' and 'more pertinent' than the German or Italian reformists, while de Man praises Mussolini for his appreciation of Sorel, creative force, dynamism and possession of the 'eternally revolutionary forces of the spirit'.[24] Sorel and de Man illustrate precisely the dangers of a moralistic approach to socialist politics and a celebration of non-rational action, vitalism and the will. For in making this move they abandon any rational argument regarding the social and economic purpose for violence in favour of what amounts to little more than 'fascist prattle' (Sartre) about the nature and universal existence of violence.[25] The point is crucial for understanding the politics of the revolt against positivism generally, and the relationship between the revolutionary revision of Marxism and fascism especially. There is a certain tendency among some liberal and conservative scholars to blur the categorical distinctions between Marxism and fascism. As with the concept of totalitarianism, the fact that some writers moved from Marxism to fascism assists in the attempt to present Marxism and fascism as equally the bad guys of the twentieth century.[26] This approach may help sell books at the end of the 'age of extremes', but the vacuous belief that there is little difference between Marxism and fascism obscures the extent to which the revision of Marx abandoned categories crucial to the communist project. It therefore seriously undermines the attempt to understand fascism.

The politics of the revolt against positivism rests on a radical intensification of the debate with Marx's ghost. Pre-empting much of what is to be argued in this book, we can say that concepts central to a critical theory of society – class, history, revolution – were abandoned, and their replacements – nation, nature, war – were the crisis symptoms of bourgeois consciousness. Abandoning the concept of class and class struggle, fascism masquerades as the representative of all classes, conceived as a single national unit; fascism obliterates history from politics and fills the space with nature; fascism appropriates the concept of revolution, applies it to its own activism, and declares revolution to be nothing other than one manifestation of the universal war.

The will to universal war

Mussolini's own intellectual trajectory is illustrative of the above comments. History, for Mussolini, is a process of struggle, undertaken by collective forces; this much he could adopt from Marx. But for struggle to take place what is needed is for groups to feel a sense of community, to identify with their collective in a sentimental fashion and to be led by a strong leader.[27] For the struggling group to be successful a vanguard or revolutionary elite is necessary. This vanguard is expected to exploit collective sentiment and help energize its will. In its adoption of Nietzschean arguments, Bergsonian

language and Le Bon's psychological meanderings, Mussolini's
revision of Marxism followed Sorel's – away from bourgeois liberal
pacifism *à la* Bernstein and towards a transformation of the
revolutionary class struggle of classical Marxism into one aspect of
the will to power, rooted in a vitalist conception of group energy:
'The classic conception of revolution finds in today's trend of
philosophic thought an element of vitality. Our conception rejuven-
ates.' As with the reformist revision of Marxism, the movement is
everything for Mussolini, but for very different reasons: as struggle,
the movement is 'life' itself. As Ernst Nolte puts it, when Mussolini
exclaims 'what life, what enthusiasm, what force in our ranks', he
comes close to the borderline where Marxism ends and 'life-
philosophy' begins. Until the First World War and the Russian
revolution he did not fully cross this line, but by 1920 he had, in
effect, abandoned Marx for Nietzsche.[28] In the 1922 article 'Which
Way Is the World Going?', for example, he claims that whereas the
nineteenth century worshipped matter, the twentieth century will
worship the spirit, and this return of spiritual values is to be a
philosophical break with the pseudo-scientific determinism of
socialism.[29]

The centrality of 'life-philosophy' and the will to power is
revealed in virtually every sentence of the 1932 'Doctrine of
Fascism', written with Gentile. Fascism establishes itself 'against
the flabby materialistic positivism of the nineteenth century . . .
Fascism desires an active man, one engaged in activity with all his
energies: it desires a man virilely conscious of the difficulties that
exist in action'. Because fascism is equally 'opposed to all the
individualistic abstractions of a materialist nature' it posits human
beings as individuals only in so far as they coincide with the state,
which, in turn, is rooted in the concept of life and rests on an
intuition of an organic vision. And in the fascist concept of the state,
the state is a will to power.[30] This concept of the will constitutes a
dominant philosophical principle in fascism. The same conception
informs virtually all of Hitler's speeches and writings, from his more
'philosophical' moments to his attempt to control the army. As J.P.
Stern notes, despite a far weaker knowledge than Mussolini, of
Nietzsche in particular and political philosophy more generally,
Hitler knew the political value of making the vocabulary of the will
his own, turning it into a metaphysical abstraction which, given its
vacuity, can explain everything. The prerequisite for success of the

German nation in its struggle against the defeat of 1918 was 'not arms, as [the] bourgeois "statesmen" keep prattling, but the forces of the will'.[31] And on 20 May 1943, when Hitler was once more criticizing his generals for failing to do what they regarded as impossible – the Hermann-Goering Division could not be moved to the mainland from Sicily in time for the Allied invasion, they insisted, because of the ferries – Hitler retorted: 'It's not the ferries that are decisive. What is decisive is the Will!'.[32] Indeed, the success of national socialism in Germany was read and presented by Nazi propaganda as the 'Triumph of the Will'.

Two of the central features of fascism follow from the rejection of reason and intellect and their replacement by the will and spirit, though they are both rooted in the same fascist mentality. The first is the rejection of theory, and the second is the conceptualization of politics and society as a realm of permanent struggle and war.

For fascism, theoretical systems only serve to forestall wilful action. The stress on doctrine and theoretical work is part of the decadence of bourgeois life, a means by which boredom reigned supreme. When Italy's best-known poet and novelist, Gabriele D'Annunzio, established occupation of Fiume with a new concept of life and a break with both capitalism and socialism (an act that was to have a dramatic effect on Mussolini's own understanding of fascism), one of his reasons was that unless something was done we would all die of boredom. Likewise, for Mussolini 'the Fascist disdains the "comfortable" life'.[33] And because for fascism human beings are essentially irrational, theory fails to act as a mobilizing force; it is not Marxist *theory* that mobilizes socialists, but wilful action on the part of leaders.

Anti-rationalism passes over into an anti-intellectualism. Being based on abstract principles and the concept of 'humankind', intellectualism obliterates questions of collective identity and ignores the importance of *roots*, as we shall see, and thus destroys the human spirit. Maurice Barrès attacked the intellectuals' protest over the Dreyfus affair on the grounds that intellectuals convince themselves that society should be founded on the basis of reason, that is, free from prejudice; they fail to see that it in fact rests on past exigencies that may be foreign to the individual reason. Kantianism, 'the state ethic of France', encourages us to lay down rules for 'humankind' seen as an abstract universal entity, and thus has no sense in which men are rooted in soil, history and the nation.

Caught up in mere words a child is cut off from all reality: Kantian doctrine uproots him from the soil of his ancestors. A surplus of diplomas creates what we may call . . . a 'proletariat of graduates'. This is our indictment of the universities: what happens to their product, the intellectual, is that he becomes an enemy of society.

Likewise, Gottfried Benn, the most important poet of the Nazi period, attacked those writers who 'sit next to ministers at banquets, a carnation in their button-hole, five wine-glasses set out for their use, and sign petitions about the problems of the age'. Gentile regarded the intellectual man of letters as a bastard product of the Italian Renaissance, searching for the pros and cons of situations and thus remaining a permanent apathetic spectator, refusing to commit himself to the struggle. 'All passion dies in his breast and he shuns the streets where people are fighting, suffering and dying and stands watching in safety'.[34] The purpose of disparaging 'intellectuals' in this way is to obliterate what fascism regards as their *modus operandi*: the search for truth through the use of reason. For fascism, one should ask not which doctrine is true, but adopt whatever belief expresses the will most forcefully and is most likely to mobilize the masses. Action, not thought, will be the basis of individual and social transformation. In that sense fascism, for fascists, is not a theory to be understood, but a universal principle the vitality of which can be *felt* by anyone; its vitality is its truth. By divorcing thought from action and concentrating entirely on the former, intellectuals glorify theory and thus denigrate the vital nature and energy of action. Theoretical systems are prisons, restricting the movement of will.

This rejection of theory in favour of practice does not entail a rejection of *thought per se*, however, but represents fascism's understanding of itself as *faith*, that is, as the equivalent of a *religion* rather than a (rational) doctrine. Because people need to believe rather than to understand, the conceptual framework of fascism must be articulated in language and symbolism closer to that found in religion rather than rationalism. Hence the insistence of Mussolini and Gentile in 'The Doctrine of Fascism' that, despite the focus on action, fascism *is* a system of thought, but a religious one: 'fascism is a religious conception in which man is seen in his immanent relationship with a superior law and with an objective Will that transcends the particular individual and raises him to conscious membership of a spiritual society'. Fascism is a faith, a spiritualized conception; the state, for Mussolini and Gentile, assumes the status of a deity: 'the Fascist State . . . is a force, but a spiritual force . . . It is the soul of the soul'.[35] In the case of Nazism, the 'revolution of the spirit' which the Nazi revolution was intended to be was founded on a 'spiritual conception of a general nature', as Hitler put it. Alfred Rosenberg's concept of race in his account of the 'myth of the twentieth century' is rooted in his concept of 'race-soul', a *Volk* that is 'primarily religiously-oriented':

> The life of a race does not represent a logically-developed philosophy nor even the unfolding of a pattern according to natural law, but rather the development of a mystical synthesis, an activity of soul, which cannot be explained rationally.[36]

Thinking of fascism as religion enables interesting reinterpretations of various fascist phenomena: the leadership cult, for example, assumes the air of religious devotion – the fascist leader being analogous to the Pope in the Catholic Church – and expulsion from the party (in the case of Italy) meant expulsion from public life and thus the equivalent of excommunication.[37] But my concern here is the way in which this affects the fascist confrontation with rationalism and materialism. Fascism's attack on both rationalism and materialism is motivated by the fact that both necessarily undermine religious conceptions and arguments. But the 'religion' of fascism is far from the Judaeo-Christian tradition; indeed, it undermines that very tradition. The religion of fascism rests on a sanctification of nature and the nation. In fascist thought the 'laws of nature' are simultaneously scientifically verifiable and mystified. The resulting *biological mysticism* appears to have both the status of science and the power of religion. To mobilize the masses in an anti-communist fashion, fascism 'nationalizes' the masses, that is, reconstitutes the working class as part of the nation, presenting the struggle of the nation in terms of a mysticism of nature: the nation in motion fulfils its historic role by realizing its natural spirit – the will to power. It is in this conjunction of nature and the nation – categories central to fascism and which therefore dominate the chapters which follow – that war is crucial. As Walter Benjamin puts it: 'In the parallelogram of forces formed by . . . nature and the nation – war is the diagonal'.[38] War sustains the dynamic of nature and contributes to the power of the nation.

Once again the Nietzschean will to power is important. Anyone 'who has pondered on the order of this world realizes that its meaning lies in the warlike survival of the fittest', Hitler tells us.[39] Because this is so it is only the fittest – those who express the will to power most categorically and forcefully – who will survive. Rejecting the importance of theory leaves one only with practice. But without any connection to actual principles, thought through and defended on theoretical grounds, practice – action – becomes an end in itself. And because practice is the will to power, it is necessarily about struggle, and a violent one at that. In this the insistence on war as the highest achievement of civilization becomes crucial. Nowhere is this clearer than in the work of the futurists and their political and cultural influence. In the 'Manifesto of Futurism' (1909) Marinetti declares the 'love of danger, the habit of energy . . . courage, audacity and revolt'. This struggle is not only a struggle for power, but is equally the expression of an aesthetic ideal. 'Except in struggle, there is no more beauty. No work without an aggressive character can be a masterpiece'; the consequence of this is that futurism will 'glorify war – the world's only hygiene'.[40] Fascism follows suit: 'War alone brings up to their highest tension all human energies and puts the stamp of nobility upon the peoples who have the courage to meet it'.[41]

Now, such a formulation may appear consistent with the centrality of war to European social and political thought generally. Many writers indeed glorify war – Nietzsche's paean to the 'masterpiece' that is war and his insistence that great politics requires war and war again, and Joseph de Maistre's praise of war as divine spring immediately to mind.[42] And crucial to the formation of fascist thought, especially in France, was their appreciation and appropriation of Proudhon's understanding of the sublime character of war.[43] It is not only the reactionary tradition which understood the importance of war. Marxism also points to the importance of war in the process of revolution and emancipation – the class war being the obvious one, but also national wars more generally as part of the momentum towards revolutionary change – and writers central to the liberal tradition, such as Kant, also point to the ubiquitous nature of war despite their demand for perpetual peace. Yet it is seriously misleading to suggest, as Noël O'Sullivan does, that fascism's cult of struggle, violence and war did not mark a radical departure from the previous European tradition.[44] Claims that 'civilization is nothing but the glory of incessant struggle'

(D'Annunzio)[45] may sound like the opening claim in *The Communist Manifesto* – that the history of all hitherto existing society is the history of class struggle – or the concluding comment in *The Poverty of Philosophy* – that we are faced with combat or death, bloody struggle or extinction – but the similarity is entirely superficial. For fascism, violence and war are *absolutes*. D'Annunzio is praising struggle *for its own sake*, not for the outcome it may achieve.

It is because fascism glorifies war for its own sake that the fascist revels in the fact that there is no need to give any reason for war, no need to fight a war for rational principles or social and political causes. The glories it brings are not from its achievements – a future classless society in which war is eliminated, say – but from the struggle itself. The claim of the conservative revolutionary, Ernst Jünger, that 'where authentic passion breaks through – above all, in the naked and immediate struggle for life and death – it becomes a matter of secondary importance in which century, for what ideas, and with what weapons the battle is being fought' is echoed throughout all fascist writings, which become mere fables of aggression.[46] In *Mein Kampf* Hitler insists that when nations fight, all humanitarian concepts crumble into nothingness; whereas for Valois in France, war, 'the primary law of life', is 'the only way of achieving the highest plane of [the] life instinct' and thus realizes the will to power. As the 'beautiful crossfire of hatred and love' (Maurras) war presents us with moments of extreme peril and is thus of *elemental* and *existential* significance.[47] In this sense fascism *aestheticizes* war. As Benjamin notes, 'it is symptomatic that the same boyish rapture that leads to a cult, to an apotheosis of war . . . is nothing other than an uninhibited translation of the principles of *l'art pour l'art* to war itself'.[48] There is nothing in Marxism or liberalism that is similar. The Kantian belief in the search for 'perpetual peace' and the socialist declaration of 'war on war' are obliterated, only to be replaced by the Nietzschean demand for perpetual war, or 'war and war again', an idea and image of war which is a specifically fascist reverie.[49] In this sense war constitutes the fascist universal.

Fascism saw the First World War as a crucial historical moment, a turning point in history where history refused to turn.[50] The unfavourable political settlement in the period after 1918, combined with the strength of communist movements across Europe, only added to the humiliation of being unable to build on the

camaraderie experienced in the trenches and the dignity of sacrifice
and death that the war allowed. But the cult of the fallen soldier, the
myth of the war experience and the importance of what Mussolini
called the 'trenchocracy' should be traced as much to the role of war
as the fascist universal as to the concrete specificity of the First
World War.[51] In reality there is only one war for fascism, the
universal 'war', of which all particular wars – the world war, the race
war, the war against communism – are but momentary and limited
parts. The importance of war lies in the conjunction of war as an
inner experience, as the highest form of political activity, and as the
supreme application of modern technology. The subjectivism of the
front soldier's experience of annihilation is transformed into the
objectivist affirmation of a metaphysical-vitalist strength shaped by
fate.[52] War shapes man's spiritual character and is the defining
characteristic of nature. The state of war is thus the universal norm;
this means that there is no real distinction between politics and war.
But this means in turn that actual physical combat, the attempted
destruction of human life through the total mobilization of the
nation, is the entelechy of fascism.

'First: *I Became a Nationalist*'

The stress on perpetual war raises questions concerning the nature of the collective subject engaging in war. The answer is found in the nation. Moreover, once the nation is posited as the true subject of war, it can then be presented as the grounds for a 'classless' society. Put simply: the nation occupies a central place in fascism. It is fascist *nationalism* which facilitates the break with liberal and Marxist universalism and, in the case of the latter, its identification of internationalism as the key to class struggle. In this chapter I first outline the importance of nationalism to fascism (which I develop further in Chapter 3), before making some more general comments on the nature of the fascist 'nation' and its relationship with race and state. I shall argue that the differences within fascism concerning the nature of the state and the extent of the stress on race should not lead us to reject the use of the concept of fascism beyond the Italian example.

From class in struggle to nation at war

Mussolini's early Marxism meant that he frequently adopted an internationalist line. In 1912 he was insisting that 'We cannot conceive of a patriotic socialism. Socialism is truly of a panhuman and universal nature . . . there are only two fatherlands in the world, that of the exploited and that of the exploiters'. Yet in the 'Naples Speech', three days before the 1922 March on Rome, he was claiming that 'we have created our myth . . . Our myth is the nation, our myth is the greatness of the nation'.[1] Such a shift encourages the belief that the First World War (WWI) was the key historical event which transformed Mussolini the socialist into Mussolini the nationalist and from there into a fascist. Mussolini himself claimed that the entry of Italy into the war marked the beginning of the fascist revolution,[2] and the cult of the fallen soldier and the myth of the great war lend weight to such claims. Moreover, Mussolini was heavily influenced by the nationalist sentiment across Italy and Europe before, during and after WWI. The birth of organized fascism in Italy on 23 March 1919 also encourages us to think of fascism as in some sense an *outcome* of WWI. But the common claim that Mussolini's shift into fascism via a conversion to nationalism occurred *after* and *because* of the war obscures the importance of Mussolini's pre-war nationalism and, in turn, the importance to this of the revolt against positivism and the revision of Marxism.

The section of the Naples Speech in which Mussolini presents the nation as fascism's central concern is illustrative of these origins. Mussolini sustains his claim in the following way:

> We have created our myth. The myth is a *faith*, a *passion*. It is not necessary for it to be a reality. It is a reality in the sense that it is a *stimulus*, is *hope*, is *faith*, is *courage*. Our myth is the nation, our myth is the greatness of the nation! . . . For us the nation is not just territory, but *something spiritual* . . . A nation is great when it translates into reality *the force of its spirit*.[3]

The language here – of vitalism and spirit – posits myth as the means for the nation to mobilize, a hope behind which mass action occurs and which stimulates the masses into courageous acts. Because its unity is a spiritual one, beyond mere geography and population, it is not open to rational analysis. But this conceptualization of the nation in fact existed in Mussolini's work well before the experience of WWI. Prior to the war he often used nationalist language even as he was insisting on the importance of an internationalist class analysis, and A. James Gregor is probably right to claim that a revolutionary nationalism was already present in Mussolini's work by 1909.[4] The crucial point, however, is that this nationalism rested on his adoption of the language of the intellectual culture at the time; his concept of the nation after WWI was formed through language and concepts inspired by his earlier reading of Nietzsche, Sorel and Le Bon, and his concept of revolutionary nationalism was rooted in his understanding of the importance of national sentiment and, within this, the emotional forces thought to tie a person to the nation. Undoubtedly in his early career Mussolini still considered interests to be defined by class, which thereby formed the principal ground of social identity, but this did not mean that no other collective sentiments existed. Indeed, it was frequently these other sentiments which proved to be the mobilizing force behind mass action.

The question Mussolini faced was how to resolve the possible tension between nationalism, albeit one conceived as revolutionary, and a socialism which by definition made the distinction between oppressive and oppressed classes, proletariat and bourgeois, the primary social and political division. The answer lay in the key similarity he thought he found between socialist and nationalist goals: their joint commitment to the modernization of Italy. Because national development meant, in effect, industrial development, and because socialism was to depend on the most advanced industrial development possible, nationalist and socialist goals could be combined within the modernization of the nation. The demand for the development of the nation *vis-à-vis* other nations could thus incorporate the demand for socialist development. Instead of class war, revolutionary social change would be brought about through the war of nations. Likewise, national sentiment could thus be read as incorporating socialist 'sentiment'. In essence, Mussolini followed an increasing number of writers[5] in effecting a shift in the concept of the oppressed group. Instead of identifying the proletariat as the oppressed class and emancipation from bourgeois domination as its goal, Italy was presented as a proletarian nation and emancipation from bourgeois nations, the goal. The proletariat had a (socialist) investment in the advance of the nation.

The outbreak of war in 1914 gave this approach to the nation an important historical and political thrust. The war was taken to reveal not only the centrality of the nation over classes but also the paucity of the internationalism held by the Socialist International. The collapse of hitherto explicitly Marxist parties and organizations in the face of WWI only served to confirm the nation as the prime subject and object of struggle. Socialism, it appeared, had given way to nationalism. The Socialist International was dead, and one of the reasons for its death was the indifference it had shown to the problem of nations. The struggle for working-class emancipation had been usurped by a struggle of greater importance – the emancipation of the nation. In this sense, WWI confirmed the world-historical role of the nation. It is not so much that WWI saw the transformation of Mussolini from socialism to nationalism (and from there to fascism), but that whereas before the war he had couched his nationalism in socialist terminology, after 1919 the socialist terminology is slowly dissolved into categories central to nationalism. This makes more sense of his adoption of crowd psychology, for it is sentiment for the nation rather than rational adherence to socialist demands which provide the basis for social action. Superficially this did not mean that the struggle for proletarian emancipation was by-passed, but that it was incorporated into the national struggle in a national socialist synthesis, through what Hitler described as the *nationalization of the masses*.[6] Dissolving class into nation, however, transforms the agent of revolution from the proletariat to the nation. The proletariat is ousted from its place as the subject of history and replaced with the nation, conceptualized as a radically aggressive historical subject, geared for war and binding its population through sentimental attachment. With this, fascism is born.

Fascism, then, deifies the nation. This development in Mussolini's intellectual and political commitments occurred in almost all of those who would make important contributions to fascism, regardless of whether they started their political life as Marxists or other kinds of socialists. In France this included Georges Sorel, Henrik de Man, Maurice Barrès, Marcel Déat, Georges Valois and Pierre Drieu La Rochelle; Doriot's Parti Populaire Française subscribed to a full-blown integral nationalism. Britain's premier fascist, Oswald Mosley, was to declare that 'if you love your country you are a nationalist, and if you love your people you are a socialist. Put the two together and you have National Socialism'. In Italy, along with Gentile and Mussolini, it included Vilfredo Pareto, A. Labriola and Enrico Corradini. Key German fascists, such as Alfred Rosenberg and Walther Darré, made the same intellectual and political move, and Hitler is clear about the formative moment in his politicization: 'First: *I became a nationalist*'.[7]

Grasping the centrality of the nation and nationalism is thus crucial for our understanding of fascism. As Tom Nairn puts it, 'it was here [in Germany and Italy] that nationalism was carried to its "logical conclusion"'. Nairn's point is that fascism, seen in sufficient *historical* depth, tells us more about nationalism than any other episode.[8] But two issues immediately confront us. First, there is the relationship between Nazism and fascism as articulated by non-Nazi writers. Put simply: is Nazism a bona fide version of fascism? Those who deny that it is rest their case on the biological racism central to Nazism but not to 'fascism proper', so to speak. The issue of race is often said to make it impossible to treat Nazism as part of fascism.[9] As Tim Mason puts it, it is Nazi racism that always threatens to shatter generic concepts of fascism.[10] Second, there is the relationship between fascism, socialism and Marxism. In placing the nation at its heart, fascism seeks to integrate the working class into the nation. Fascist 'socialism' is to be a socialism for 'the people' and not just for the proletariat. This second issue is double-edged. On the one hand, does the emergence of a 'national socialism' signal the shift from the left to the right of the political spectrum and thus confirm fascism as a phenomenon of the right, or is fascism somehow 'beyond left and right'? On the other hand, by what mechanism does the incorporation of the working class take place; that is, what is the fascist 'solution' to the issue of class struggle, and does this make fascism a genuine 'third way' between the capitalism of the right and the socialism of the left? In the argument that follows, I attempt an answer to some of these questions. In the process, I decline the open invitation to give up thinking of Nazism as a variety of fascism. It is in conjunction with the nation that race, state and class are understood differently by different types of fascist. It is therefore only with this conjunction that we can grasp the importance of state and race in fascist arguments. The remainder of this chapter focuses on the role of the nation and attempts a provisional explanation of the biological racism and anti-Semitism in Nazism. The argument is developed further in the following chapters, where the relationship between fascism, capitalism and modernity is addressed and fascism presented as a 'revolution against the revolution'.

Imagined communities: the universal state and the racial nation

One of the problems that the emergent fascist movement faced in Italy was the absence of a genuine Italian national myth, despite the movement's own invocation of the myth of the nation. The historic reasons for this lie in Italy's failure to become a nation-state until 1861, a major reason for which was the myth of Rome, embodied in the papacy, and its ubiquitous spiritual challenge to national liberation movements. As J.L. Talmon notes:

> the myth of the unique and at the same time universal significance of Rome was so deeply embedded in the Italian mind that the claim to secular, national self-determination seemed a poor, inadequate, indeed demeaning challenge in comparison with the myth of the universal church, the heir of the imperial myth.[11]

In this context two features of the way Italian fascists understood the nation and state become crucial. First, the nation had to be *created*, and the only force which could create it was the state. In contrast to the nineteenth-century view of states as the creation of nations, Mussolini and Gentile insist that 'it is not the nation that generates the State [but that] the nation is created by the State'. Second, this conception of the state is necessarily a *spiritual* one. The state is a higher, ethical, universal reality. 'The Fascist State, the highest and most powerful form of personality, is a force, but a spiritual force, which takes over all the forms of the moral and intellectual life of man.'[12] The myth of the nation and the rebirth of the Italian nation, for Italian fascists, thus required the creation of the nation by a universal force which could challenge the moral and spiritual power of the Church. For this reason the state had to assume the guise of a new spiritual community alternative to the power of the Church. The state, then, is a moral unity. Yet if the nation displaces the proletariat as the agent of revolution, and the nation has to be created by the state, the state in effect becomes the agent of the revolution and the subject of history, its task being to unite the nation into a higher ethical order.

This demand for an ethical state incorporating the moral and political unity of the people enables fascism to transform the discourse of liberal and social democracy into the discourse of state power, circumventing fundamental problems of liberal democracy by subsuming them under the idea of the ethical state. 'The Doctrine of Fascism' overcomes any liberal hand-wringing over the relationship between individual liberty and state power by rede-fining liberty as a property of the higher personality of the state. If 'liberty is to be the attribute of the real man, and not that abstract puppet envisaged by individualistic Liberalism, Fascism is for liberty'. The individual is free in so far as he is part of the state, and only free where he is part of the state. 'In this sense the Fascist State is totalitarian', but this totalitarianism is the highest freedom for the individual.[13] As a personality in its own right, the ethical reality of the nation, *the state is an end in itself.* Now, there is no such conception of the state in Nazism. In many ways the Nazi concept of the state is diametrically opposed to the Italian fascist one, treating the state as a 'monstrosity' to be overcome in a higher order but which can none the less be used as a means to an end, the end being a higher racial formation and racial superiority. For Hitler, 'there can be no such thing as state authority as an end in itself . . . the highest aim of human existence is not the preservation of a state, let alone a government, but the preservation of the species'.[14] Indeed, Nazi writers often sought to distance themselves from the concept of the state found in Italian fascism. Describing the 'revolution' of 30 January 1933 as a break with the old absolutist conception of the state, Alfred Rosenberg argues that the state is to be an instrument of the national socialist movement rather than a total state to be worshipped in its own right. With one eye clearly on Italy, he claims that 'If we continue to speak of the total state, younger National Socialists and coming generations will gradually shift the state concept into the centre of things'. In contrast, it is the national socialist movement, moulded for the collective German *Volk*, which should be at the heart of the theory and practice of Nazism.[15]

Here the very different history of Germany needs to be recognized. The linguistic and cultural unity that existed in Germany meant that it already had a nation to speak of. As Roger Griffin points out, the fact that Germany existed as a *Kulturnation* long before it became a *Staatsnation* meant that those responding to the decadence they felt was overwhelming Germany could point to a glorious past rooted in collective solidarity. Their destiny was thus to struggle for the reconstitution of the organic community.

> The word *Volk*, and especially its adjectival form *völkisch*, thus became endowed with untranslatable connotations of racial solidarity and collective mission. In its radical forms, moreover, *völkisch* thought implied that the nation was endowed with a mysterious essence which could be sapped by such 'decadent' forces as socialism, materialism, cosmopolitanism and internationalism.[16]

The way was thus open for some German nationalists to struggle not so much for the nation, but to defend the nation on the grounds of *völkisch* purity. In the biological racism which this gives rise to, the state is but a means to an end: the preservation of the race.

How is it then that race and, relatedly, anti-Semitism, are so central to Nazism? And does this mean that fascism and Nazism are two separate and distinguishable ideologies? One response to these questions has been to identify a peculiarly German mode of thought which fed into Nazi ideology and explains the centrality of biological racism and anti-Semitism to Nazism. This is the explanation given by Mosse: 'The divergence of German fascism from the other fascisms reflects the difference between German thought and that of the other western European nations'. Some writers, such as Hermann Glaser, posit the roots of national socialism in German culture, while others resort to a combination of such claims: Daniel Jonah Goldhagen, for example, understands Nazi anti-Semitism as a result of the 'cultural cognitive model' of German society and the 'common sense' of German thought and culture.[17] It is undoubtedly the case that *völkisch* ideas were widespread intellectual currency in Germany and contained potential political force. As Fritz Stern makes clear in his study of the politics of cultural despair and the rise of 'Germanic' ideology, the fear was that modernity – the rise of democracy, rationalism and the legacy of the French revolution – threatened this idealized unity. The revival of *völkisch* unity was meant to be the antidote to modern decadence.[18] In the historical conditions of atomization, alienation and decadence, this idealized unity could become politically pertinent. In other words, under certain conditions *völkisch* ideas could take on a forceful, even revolutionary pertinence, and did so for the political right. After WWI some 75 *völkisch* groups existed in Germany during Weimar, with the old Conservative and Free Conservative parties reconstituting themselves as the Deutschnationale Volkspartei (DNVP, or German National People's Party) in the aftermath of WWI and the failed German revolution.[19] But is this permeation by *völkisch* ideas enough to explain Nazism in Germany and its distinguishing feature of biological racism and anti-Semitism? To get to grips with this we need to go further into the political power of *völkisch* ideas.

Here we need to address the question of race. Extending a point made by Peter Gay, we can say that race was everywhere by the end of the nineteenth century, saturating social, political and scientific thought. Yet however much those who spoke of race thought (and still think) they were engaged in a purely scientific activity, even 'the most neutral use of the word "race" could not conceal the invidious element lurking in the background', namely, their contribution to the cultivation of hatred.[20] For the purpose of differentiating between races is never simply to show that races exist, that is, that there are human groups whose members possess common physical characteristics. Nor is it to show that there is a continuity between physical type and character and that individual behaviour depends on the racial group to which the individual belongs. It is in fact to politicize the pseudo-scientific activity by ranking the races hierarchically and reworking political structures such that institutions and processes which depend on and support racial differences are maintained and strengthened. With this last point racial theory joins racist practice.[21] However much the argument turned on the scientific measurement of skulls and other physical characteristics, all commentators agreed that what was carried in the blood was a set of characteristics and capacities linking individuals in some indefinable way, some mystical fashion, to other members of their race. What racism produces – *völkisch* or otherwise – is, in essence, a *biological mysticism*.

The Nazis took these ideas and gave them a political charge that they otherwise lacked, in two ways. First, the Nazis sought to go beyond *völkisch* groups by grounding the racism of their ideas in a strong conception of movement and party. The reason for grounding the movement in a National Socialist German Workers' Party (NSDAP) was that the party form would also serve to frighten the 'folkish sleepwalkers' away. Left on their own, the Nazis believed, *völkisch* ideas are like religious conceptions of the world: spiritually powerful but politically nebulous and without any organizational means for realizing their force. For Hitler, the concept *völkisch* was 'unclearly defined': 'in view of its conceptual boundlessness [the idea] is no possible basis for a movement'. What was needed was an instrument which would enable the *völkisch* world-view to fight, a militant organization willing to mobilize the masses and produce the necessary leadership. Second, the struggle between races was seen as a struggle of the eternal will for superiority, serving the aristocratic principle of nature. The state would be the means to the preservation of this inequality and the racial foundation of society.[22]

Now, there are several issues at stake here. First, there is the claim that Nazi biological racism and anti-Semitism reflects a

substantial difference between German and non-German thought
and culture. The problem with such a claim is that it rests on a
simplistic distinction between styles of *national* thought. Clearly
völkisch thought had a resonance in Germany that it failed to
achieve elsewhere, but there are dangers in reducing it to something
peculiarly German. As Geoff Eley points out, until 1914 the term
Volk had the same double connotations of 'national' and 'popular'
found in other countries as well,[23] and a large number of the
contributors who assisted in turning *völkisch* thought into virulent
racism were non-German. Admittedly Arthur de Gobineau, who
made racial doctrine popular with his *Essay on the Inequality of the
Human Races* (1853–5), was more widely read in Germany than in
his native France (hence the creation of the Gobineau Society in
Germany), and Houston Stuart Chamberlain, whose *Foundations
of the Nineteenth Century* (1898–1900) combined racial science with
a mysticism and a political programme, was of English origin but
identified with the Germans and was taken up by them in return.[24]
But this hardly justifies the claim that there is something specific in
German thought and culture which enables us to explain the role of
racism and anti-Semitism in fascism.[25]

   The approach to Nazism which tries to explain it with reference
to 'German thought', 'German culture', 'German militarism',
'German authoritarianism', 'the German cultural cognitive model
of society', or, for that matter, anything else deemed the essence of
'the German character', runs the risk of perpetuating the myth of
German peculiarity, the idea that Nazism was the outcome of a
German deviation from an otherwise 'normal' type of European
development.[26] Such an approach not only fails to grasp the
essential relation between Nazism and other forms of fascism, but
also obliterates the important exchange of ideas that occurred
across Europe and contributed to the success of fascism. Moreover,
such arguments concede to fascism its own central claim: that
nations are natural phenomena which shape our character and
which thus determine our place in history. Rejecting the claim that
Nazism can be understood through German peculiarity does not
mean that one makes no reference to historical specificity; it *does*,
however, mean that our major conceptual tool for the understanding of fascism is not reduced to national 'peculiarities'.

   The question, then, is how to incorporate the phenomenon of
Nazism and its biological racism and anti-Semitism into the account

of fascism being developed here. One way is through the idea of the nation and the virulent nationalism found in fascist thought. In Hitler's *Mein Kampf* there is a continual oscillation between race and nation, as though distinguishing between them makes no difference. In the Chapter on 'Nation and Race' he distinguishes between 'culture-bearing' and 'culture-creating' *races*, only to refer to them later as culture-bearing and culture-creating *nations*, a transition made via the concept of a 'people'. Sometimes his oscillation between the two results in both being reduced to the blood. Indeed, Clause 4 of the Programme of the German Workers' Party as it was transformed into the NSDAP in February 1920 states that 'Only members of the nation may be citizens of the State. Only those of German blood, whatever their creed, may be members of the nation'.[27] And early Nazi ideologues such as Walther Darré wrote that 'the choice is now between nationalism and internationalism; that is, between anti-semitism and pro-semitism'.[28]

Hitler's oscillation between race and nation is not surprising given his prime propaganda technique of reducing everything to one simple proposition, but there is more than propaganda at stake here. *Volk* is a notoriously slippery concept, shifting as it does between 'people', 'nation' and a 'natural' racial community of blood and soil (which are, in turn, all equally slippery). The oscillation masks the fact that *nationalism* is the real driving force behind Nazism, as it is with fascism in general. The precondition of the existence of a higher racial humanity is not the state but the nation; thus the importance of the state lies in the relative utility it possesses for the nation.[29] Moreover, when Hitler talks about the nation, he frequently does so in language that would not be out of place in Mussolini and Gentile's account of the state: 'the underlying idea is to do away with egoism and to lead people into the sacred collective egoism which is the nation'.[30]

As a political programme Nazism set itself against the Weimar Republic, the Marxist and social democratic left, unemployment and economic collapse, and the Versaille Treaty. In this it shared the ideological ground with the range of conservative, reactionary and counter-revolutionary forces on the political right generally. In Weimar Germany these forces often took the form of *völkisch* organizations or parties. As a political force Nazism had to appeal to these groups as well as rally the masses. To do this it frequently invoked nationalism rather than racism for, despite their *völkisch*

character and the 'nebulous abstraction' (as Griffen calls it), of a
rejuvenated *Volk* at the centre of their thought, the central thread
connecting all the groups on the political right in Weimar Germany was *nationalism*. In Arthur Moeller van den Bruck's *The
Third Reich*, for example, it is German nationalism that is the
means of expressing German universalism, for it will enable the
Third Reich to be a genuine 'third way' between capitalism and
socialism. This third way will be achieved by incorporating the
proletariat through a return to the values of the *Volk*, to be established by making the proletariat part of the nation. This approach
is representative of the range of conservative revolutionaries who
played a crucial role in undermining Weimar democracy. Likewise, the programme of the DNVP was committed to national
rebirth in which racial origins were to be protected 'for the sake of
national unity'. Its reference to 'spiritual unity' is a reference to
the unity of the nation. Just as this nationalism was to be the
protection against Bolshevism, the solution to the crisis of Weimar
democracy and thus the saviour of Germany, so it was with
nationalism rather than racism that the Nazis sought to win the
support of both other forces and the German people.[31] This point
is developed in the next two chapters.

The same issue lies behind the racism of French fascists such as
Maurice Barrès. Insisting that the social and historical collective
force that shapes him as an individual is his race, Barrès is none
the less forced to concede that the French 'are not a race but a
nation'. But this is something he regrets: it is unfortunate that the
French are only a nation rather than a race.[32] This would appear to
separate race and nation, identifying the former as the most important mobilizing force. Yet what is a nation, for Barrès? History
and geography are its main determinants. But when discussing
nations his attention is held not by the geographical – that is, the
environmental determinant – but the historical. The historical determinant is both cultural and natural – nationality can be learned
through socialization via the range of cultural institutions geared
towards the protection and development of the nation – but is also
naturally acquired. That is, it is in our blood. And nature is always
stronger than culture – one might learn Chinese language and law
but that would not stop one from forming 'French ideas'. As Todorov puts it: 'Barrès thus constantly manipulates the metaphor of
blood, and his "nations" hardly differ from the "races" of his

contemporaries . . . Barrès's xenophobia and Judeophobia stem from his nationalism'.[33]

In one sense, then, the central issue behind racial discourse is the threat to the nation. In the case of Nazism, as the fear for the nation was transformed from *völkisch* anxiety to political programme the issue concerned not so much the question of racial intermingling as the threat posed to the nation and national unity by such intermingling. Hitler's concerns over race are in fact concerns over the racial foundations of the nation.[34] His biologism applies to the nation as to the race: it is the nation that is variously described as containing 'symptoms of disease', 'poisoning', 'creeping sickness', 'toxins', 'plague', 'parasites' and an 'alien virus'.[35] Nazism thus consolidates the centrality of nationalism to fascism by rationalizing the territoriality of some species on the natural basis of the nation-state. In Nazism the nation becomes a unit filled with blood.[36]

Thinking of nationalism's relationship to fascism in this way also partly explains the place of the Jew in Nazism. In *Mein Kampf* Hitler attacks the Jews for a variety of reasons – their conspiratorial nature, their participation in Bolshevik power and centrality to Marxism, their control of finance and capital – but the crux of his attack, and the basis of his fear, is that 'the Jew is a parasite in the body of other peoples'. This account of the Jew is founded on the fact that Jews have no home of their own, that is, the Jew is 'a parasite in the body of other nations and states'. As Hannah Arendt argues, one of the means by which the Jews are understood by Nazism, and one of the reasons why the Jews are regarded as a threat, is that the Jews are a nationless people, a non-national element in a world of nations. In other words, the Jew has no nation. The Jew is a foreigner like no other foreigner, for not only is the Jew not at home in Germany, but the Jew is not at home anywhere. Being a foreigner is the *essence* of the Jew rather than a transitory state. As such, the Jew poses a double threat. On the one hand, the Jew stubbornly refuses to adopt *the* mode of being, to adhere to *the* political form through which rootedness should be expressed. Instead the Jews insist on being a 'community' within other nations. On the other hand, being a non-national nation means that the Jews are equally an inter-national nation, in that their nationless state allows them to drift across the borders of other, real, nations. Since the nation is to be the basis of salvation, the medium through which rejuvenation and revitalization could occur, the Jews' nationless status threatens this salvation from within, so to speak.[37] Moreover, the Jew's preaching of universal human values also undermines the nation, for the Jew appears intellectually committed to a universalism which pits free will and the idea of choice – through a commitment to either universal liberal values of Enlightenment reason or Marxist internationalism – against the mythic status of national boundaries. Both physically and intellectually, the Jew defies the truth on which all nations rest their claims: the naturally ascribed character of nationhood and the naturalness of national entities.[38]

Now, I am not seeking to elide the differences between nationalism and racism; nor do I wish to reduce the latter to the former. Equally I am not arguing that racism is of no significance to our understanding of fascism. I am arguing that claims which point to the biological racism and anti-Semitism of the Nazis as the ground of a fundamental difference between Italian fascism (as 'fascism proper') and Nazism fail to register the fact that the biological racism and anti-Semitism of Nazism emerges from the xenophobic nature of nationalism. However one characterizes the distinctive feature of the kind of nationalism found in fascism – 'integral' nationalism, 'radical' nationalism and 'ultra' nationalism are all fairly common – it is the logic of nationalism and the logic of racism which share fundamental features; nationalism is *necessarily* xenophobic – that is, xenophobia is part of the logic of nationalism – and thus always remains an invitation to anti-Semitism and racism. As Peter Pulzer shows in his work on the rise of political anti-Semitism, anti-Semitism was historically a by-product of nationalism: 'nationalism had, by the beginning of the nineteenth century, become the main driving force behind anti-Semitism'.[39] In effect, the theoretical and historical roots of racism and anti-Semitism lie in nationalism.

Thinking of Nazism in this way assists in interpreting the Nazi regime itself. There has been a tendency to attribute the 'success' of Nazism to its anti-Semitism: put simply, by focusing on the Jews in particular the Nazis are said to have tapped into some kind of popular vein of resentment and encouraged the 'scapegoating' of the Jews for the ills suffered by Germans. Such an interpretation has become widespread in academic writings on Nazism and has a certain common-sense appeal. But the scapegoat thesis in fact fails to explain anything. This fact is succinctly expressed by a post-WWI joke reported by Arendt: 'An anti-semite claimed that the Jews had caused the war; the reply was: Yes, and the bicyclists. Why the bicyclists? asks the one. Why the Jews? asks the other'.[40] The scapegoat thesis has the appearance of an explanation, but in fact leaves the question begging. Historical research partially bears this out. In their campaigning and propaganda the Nazis often played down their anti-Semitism, favouring instead a focus on the import- ance of national revival – the party manifesto of 1930 insists that the party will 'allow a nation once more to rise up' and will train the nation to have an 'iron determination' so that 'in future the importance of our nation . . . corresponds to its natural worth'.[41] An analysis of the ideology of rank-and-file Nazis revealed that while those joining the party showed clear prejudices, anti- Semitism figured as the *major* prejudice in only a minority. Some 60% of activists barely mentioned anti-Semitism at all, with some even dissociating themselves from the party's anti-Semitism. This research reveals the inadequecy of explaining anti-Semitism with the scapegoat thesis. If the thesis does not apply to those inside the party, it is not likely to apply to those outside. Likewise, if the thesis has any explanatory power it must lie in being able to explain the anti-Semitism of those entering the party after 1929 in the midst of the economic crisis, when the search for a scapegoat would be at its peak. Yet it would appear that those joining the party in this period were the *least* anti-Semitic.[42] What appealed to those who sup- ported the Nazis was its ultranationalism combined with one or more of a range of other issues: anti-communism, the repeal of war reparations, the revoking of the Versailles Treaty, the curb on excessive profiteering by industry, a strong leadership to bring an end to the struggles and crises of the Weimar period and, undoubtedly for some, anti-Semitism. Arno Mayer may not be far off the mark in claiming that 'anti-Semitism did not play a decisive or even significant role in the growth of the Nazi movement and electorate'.[43]

Placing the nation and nationalism at the heart of our understand- ing of Nazi ideology is not meant to ignore the issue of race and anti-Semitism, but to give it a new theoretical direction. This would enable a rethinking of the shift to racism and anti-Semitism made by the fascist regime in Italy. It is now commonplace to claim that for the most part race was not an issue in fascism in Italy, a claim which is especially appealing to those who continue to try and separate

Nazism from fascism as a means of making fascism respectable and thus, logically, acceptable once more.[44] This rests on the general assumption that Mussolini's 'conversion' to racism and anti-Semitism in the late 1930s came about under pressure from the Nazis and was never convincing, even to most fascists, and that until the late 1930s Mussolini appeared to criticize the Nazis for their racism, arguing that fascism and national pride have no need of the 'delirium' of race.[45] The claim generally made is that racism and anti-Semitism were never done very well by the Italian fascists, supposedly because they never really believed in them. Thus even when the Italian fascist state introduced racial laws in 1938 forbidding mixed marriages and excluding Jews from military service and large landholdings, Jewish war veterans and those who had participated in the fascist movement were exempt. And Jews who could show Italian nationality were protected by Italian embassies in Nazi-occupied Europe.[46] These details are meant to show that fascist racism and anti-Semitism are some kind of aberration, due to the negative influence of the Nazis and thus nothing really to do with fascism. Thinking of anti-Semitism and racism as a by-product of nationalism, however, raises questions about such claims.

First, fascist racism and anti-Semitism in Italy were as much an outcome of a concern over the best method for policing the colonies and the necessity for justifying the domination of the colonies as they were the result of pressure from the Nazis. But the worry over the colonies was, in effect, a worry that the nation was being undermined. When in November 1938 the publication *Partito e Impero* raised questions about the role of the party given the expanded nature of the Empire following the conquest of Ethiopia, the answer it gave rested on the mobilization of the people: the function of the party is

> never to allow the Italian people to rest, to urge them on, to foster among them the urge to expand indefinitely in order to survive, to instill in them a sense of superiority of our race over the blacks . . . In short, we must try to give the Italian people an imperialist and racist mentality.

For Mussolini the necessity of stressing the domination of the Italians over the Africans was the catalyst for the development of a formal doctrine of racial superiority. Likewise, the intention behind the outlawing of conjugal relations between Italians and colonial subjects or foreigners with cultural and legal customs similar to those of the colonial subjects (April 1937), and marriages between Italian citizens of Aryan stock and members of a different race (November 1938), was to prevent the birth of racially mixed children who might pollute the Italian nation.[47] Similarly, anti-Semitism became a key issue because Mussolini identified Jewish aggression, power and corruption at the heart of the nation as a genuine concern for fascism. There followed a whole range of books debating the nature of fascist anti-Semitism and racism. But whatever differences there were between the authors of these books, they all thought of the Jewish problem in terms of the threat to the nation. *Il Popolo d'Italia*, reviewing a book by Paolo Orano in May 1937, insisted that the Jews had to decide whether they were merely guests in Italy or Italians of Jewish religion. And one solution to the Jewish problem – of being a non-national nation – presented in a government document of February 1938 and thought to have been written by Mussolini, was to create a Jewish state in some part of the world. The solution to a people existing as a state within the state was to create for them a state of their own. In other words, a racist mentality developed from the continued expansion of the nation; as with its Nazi counterpart, Italian fascist racism and anti-Semitism were the by-product of nationalism.

Second, far from becoming a pseudo-racist and anti-Semite in the late 1930s under the influence of the Nazis, Mussolini was increasingly using the language of race from 1918. As racism became more a policy of the Italian state in the late 1930s, Mussolini and other fascists justified it by claiming – correctly – that they had *always* talked of race. In April 1921, in a speech in Bologna, Mussolini claimed that 'Fascism was born . . . out of a profound, perennial need of this our Aryan and Mediterranean race' and went on to suggest that fascism sought to impart to Italians a sense of 'racial solidarity' in order to turn all Italians into 'one single pride of race'. From this point on the term 'race' appeared regularly in his writings and speeches, and the term was used widely in the writings of other Italian fascists in this period.[48] The specific use of the concept is revealing, however. For 'race' and 'racial pride' here mean very little other than 'nation' and 'national consciousness'. Hence Mussolini's claim that 'before I love the French, the English, the Hottentots, I love Italians. That is to say I love those of my own

race, those that speak my language, that share my customs, that
share with me the same history'. As Gregor notes, the racism
manifested by Mussolini in fascism's formative years was little more
than a euphoric nationalism.[49] This is equally true of his anti-
Semitism. His anti-Semitic remarks – such as his claim in 1919 that
the Jewish bankers of London and New York were bound by the
chains of race to Moscow and that 80 per cent of the leaders of the
Soviets were Jews – were commonplace in nationalist circles at the
time.[50] In other words, Mussolini became a racist and anti-Semite as
he became a nationalist and fascist.

Admittedly, Mussolini's racism and anti-Semitism appear to lack
the biologism found in Nazism, focusing instead on race formation
as a political and cultural process. But this does not mean that there
are categorical differences between Nazism and fascism. Nazi race
doctrine was in many ways remarkably unoriginal, rooted in
doctrines common in the nineteenth century. Like all doctrines,
racism has its own nuances and varieties, but to separate out
'biological' racism into a world of its own is dangerous: it
encourages the belief that some forms of racism are somehow better
or more respectable for having nothing to do with biology,
disguising the fact that all forms of racism rest on an obscure and
superficial biological reductionism in the first place.[51]

If this is the case, then what explains the place of the state and
race in Italian fascism and German Nazism is not the dominant
cultural and intellectual trajectories and milieux that existed in
those countries. Far from being the product of national peculiarity,
the concepts of state and race are different ideological mechanisms
for substantiating nationalist claims. Much of the recent and
convincing work on nationalism has pointed to the synthetic nature
of nations, to their status as imagined communities – imagined as
both inherently limited and sovereign. This has the virtue of
drawing our attention to the fact that nations are necessarily
cultural artefacts; they are imagined because members of even the
smallest nation will never know or meet their fellow members. For
nationalists this need not matter because what links us as nationals
is not our meeting or knowing but our participation in some kind of
'national spirit'. The nation supposedly links us as individuals to a
universal and collective force, of world-historical importance. As
such 'nationalism thinks in terms of historical destinies'. On this
reading, the nation has little to do with borders, forms of

government or nationality as such, but is in fact a form of community based on sentiment, emotion and instinct.[52]

For fascism the concepts of race and the universal state perform the same function. That is, the state and race in fascism work alongside the idea of the nation, combining with the nation to link the individual to a higher, spiritual and universal force. Like the nation, the race and state are imagined ethical communities in fascist thought, growing from the nation, sustaining national power against its enemies and contributing to the ideology of state power by disguising that power as a manifestation of both our 'natural' collective identity and our unity with a 'spiritual' force. To Nairn's point noted above – that, seen in sufficient *historical* depth, fascism tells us more about nationalism than any other episode – we can thus add the following: seen in sufficient *theoretical* depth, nationalism tells us a great deal about fascism.

But this begs the question: why do such imagined communities exist? Nairn writes that 'the arrival of nationalism . . . was tied to the political baptism of the lower classes' and this, it would seem, is the crux of the issue.[53] As class struggle in Europe intensified through the nineteenth and into the twentieth centuries the working class threatened to undermine national stability by bringing about a revolutionary transformation. Nationalism established itself against this historical momentum, becoming aggressively active and simultaneously mobilizing the working class behind the nation while incorporating the class into the nation. Fascism incorporates this nationalism as part of its struggle against communism. As a movement to prevent communist revolution, fascism appropriates nationalism's understanding of itself as a doctrine beyond class but none the less appropriates some of the language and concerns of socialism. It is to these issues that the following two chapters are addressed.

Revolution against the Revolution I: Capitalism, State Power and the Conservative Revolution

If the will triumphs, who loses?[1] Fascism styles itself as anti-Marxist and anti-Bolshevik, yet insists, for a variety of reasons, that it contains a commitment to socialism. The nature of 'fascist social-ism' or 'national socialism' therefore needs to be addressed. To do this I shall be rather old fashioned, which these days can only mean one thing: I shall be discussing capitalism and revolution. I shall argue that fascism appropriates socialist language, slogans and, occasionally, arguments, but by incorporating them into a broader ideological framework with nationalist, elitist and conservative intentions it dissolves socialism's key premises into a politics of reaction and, building on the work of the conservative revolution-aries, reveals itself as a counter-revolutionary phenomenon in defence of capitalism.

The argument is developed at a critical distance from the frequent claim that fascism and Marxism share common ground. A. James

Gregor's account of the 'intellectual origins of fascism' rests on the belief that fascism is a *variant* of Marxism and that both are illustrative of the 'fascist persuasion' in radical politics; a similar claim is made by Noël O'Sullivan. Even Zeev Sternhell, in his far more subtle work on the 'birth of fascist ideology', claims that fascism is a *revision* of Marxism.[2] Sternhell's joint claim that Nazism cannot be considered a form of fascism enables him to highlight the Italian case and thus the origins within Marxism of some Italian fascists, not least Mussolini. But there are a number of reasons why such an approach should be rejected. First, as soon as one incorporates German fascism into this picture it becomes difficult to sustain the exclusive focus on the revision of Marxism, given the widespread violent opposition to Marxism within the German context. Second, as a movement fascism defines itself categorically as anti-communist and anti-Marxist. Third, the term 'revision' has an ambiguity which obscures more than it reveals. The entire history of Marxism since Marx's death can in some ways be read as a series of 'revisions' of Marx in the light of theoretical critique and historical change. Can one distinguish between revisions of Marxism that remain Marxist and revisions which leave the Marxist fold? If terms such as 'Marxism' and 'fascism' (and, for that matter, liberalism, conservatism, and so on) are to retain any meaning the answer must be in the affirmative. That Marxism and fascism may share some features – an anti-parliamentarianism and commitment to radical change, for example – is less significant than the features which set them apart and place them on opposing sides of historical struggle. At the heart of this opposition lies the issue of class.

A mongrel of lies: national socialism

Despite the fact that only the Nazis included in the title of their party the designation 'National Socialist', fascism generally presents itself as socialist. We have seen how Mussolini's move out of Marxism occurred via a focus on 'proletarian nations' rather than the proletariat itself, and in the work of writers such as Corradini aggressive anti-Marxism did not preclude praising the virtues of 'national socialism' for a proletarian nation such as Italy. Maurice Barrès, in his election campaign in Nancy in 1898, coined the term 'socialist nationalism' to describe the integration of the proletariat into the nation, and Marcel Déat argued that the body of workers which stand aloof from the nation will continue to do so unless the state becomes a tool for the liberation of the proletariat, a process which would in turn enable the proletariat to arrive at the idea of the nation. For Georges Valois and Pierre Drieu La Rochelle – the former the founder of Le Faisceau and author of *French Fascism* (published in Italian in 1926), the latter the author of *Fascist Socialism* (1934) – fascism has the same aim as socialism and communism – the representation of the people – yet unlike communism it does not intend to abolish property. Instead property is to be utilized in a national framework which will harness all social forces – especially those on opposite sides of the class divide – into a national synthesis providing the basis for social justice. In this 'social nationalism' or 'national socialism', in which 'nationalism + socialism = fascism' (Valois), the state is to belong to all classes and will unite the nation with socialism.[3] For Hitler, the chief crime of Marxism is its internationalism. The way to avoid Marxists using the working class to destroy the nation is to integrate the class into the nation through the nationalization of the masses. The national socialist state will thus have no classes since classes will be united into a common framework of national unity. National prosperity will be achieved through people being bound together by a common pride and joy.[4]

What the shift to nationalism does more than anything else is to obliterate the class struggle in ideological terms. Instead of the end of class struggle through the victory of the working class and the production of a genuinely classless society, fascism ends class struggle in *this* society, that is, in class society, by dissolving the question of class *per se*. In other words, the shift in the concept of the oppressed group, explored in Chapter 2, enables fascism to 'resolve' the question of class by assuming the classlessness of class society. As Marcuse puts it:

> The whole that it [totalitarian universalism] presents is not the unification achieved by the domination of *one* class within the framework of class society, but rather a unity that combines *all* classes, that is supposed to overcome the reality of class struggle and thus of classes themselves . . . A classless society, in other words, is the goal, but a classless society on the basis of and within the framework of – the existing class society.

The purpose of this is the prevention of communism through a socialism for the nation. In practice, this is to take the form of nationalization, the direct opposite of socialization.[5] The fascist 'resolution' of the problem of class is thus a mystification; it deals with class on an ideological rather than material level. In this sense fascism reveals itself as ideology: since the fascist considers conceptions, thoughts, ideas – all the products of consciousness – as the real human chains they need fight only against these illusions of consciousness. This demand to change consciousness amounts to a demand to interpret reality in another way, that is, to recognize it by means of another interpretation.[6]

The nation is thus a concept for a new interpretation of reality, a class-ridden reality reinterpreted as classless unity. This is true of all nationalism. In fascism, however, the same is true of other key concepts such as race and state. In the case of fascist racism, for example, it is by positing fundamental differences between races and then arranging them hierarchically that the working class can be (re)presented as part of a higher race. By positing racial struggle as the driving force of history, and by pointing to the aristocratic principle in nature, the working class can be conceptualized as part of this aristocracy and part of the driving force of history. For Hitler, it is

> because of the Communists, if for no other reason, that Germany is no longer able to fight beyond its borders . . . For the nation is paralysed by class divisions. My aim is to lead the many millions of workers back to the idea of the *Volk*. That will only happen when they sincerely believe in the ideal.[7]

The message to the worker then, is: why identify with an oppressed class when you can identify with the (racial) aristocracy? Racism is thus a substitute for the class struggle, the racial other being the new enemy for the newly unified people's community. By subsuming class under a racial form the question of class struggle and the possibility of communism are obliterated. Satisfied with his own blood, the worker gives up the struggle for greater social riches.[8] The whole purpose behind *völkisch* thought is that it presents a mechanism for not only *incorporating* the working class but also *subduing* it. The working class is dangerous because, as a product of the rise of capitalism, this class more than any other embodies modern rootlessness and restlessness; as such the workers threaten the social order. If this class is given a standing in the *Volk*, the worker loses his status as an alienated proletarian and recaptures the unity of the past by being part of a new harmonious social totality; this would simultaneously be an end to social antagonism.[9] Incorporation into the *Volk* can do this because the *Volk* is the universal and spiritual unity of the German people.

In other forms of fascism the idea of the corporate state plays an almost identical role. In declaring it the *people's* state, fascism presents the state as above classes, that is, no longer under the control of one class. But it simultaneously declares that there can be nothing outside the state; that is, nothing opposed to the state. Fascism is *opposed* to socialism, claim Mussolini and Gentile, because socialism 'confines the movement of history within the class struggle and ignores the unity of classes established in one economic and morality in the State'. Fascism recognizes that divergent and opposed interests have existed, but 'wishes to bring them under the control of the State and give them a purpose within the corporative system of interests reconciled within the unity of the State'. And yet fascism also *assists* the cause of socialism by stopping it drifting down the path of communism and focusing on class struggle.[10] A similar role for the corporate state was conceived by fascists in France. Valois, for example, turned to corporatism as the basis for a renewal of social order beyond the traditional organs of labour representation. In doing so he was far from alone: Robert Soucy points out in his account of the 'first wave' of French fascism that 'every French fascist movement of the interwar period posited corporatism as the answer to Marxism'.[11]

In its focus on class Marxism conceptualizes society as fragmented and subject to internal struggle. By thinking of society as constituted as one state and one race the illusion of unity is created. Through either *Volk* or state, fascism presents its own version of totality, rooted in the nation-state. Within this totality all forms of particularity are overcome – the atomization of individuals along with the separation of classes. Fascism 'liberates' the working class by identifying it as part of the universal state or transcendent *Volk*. As such the place of the working class in history is guaranteed, but guaranteed as part of another totality; there is no need for it to struggle as a class *for itself*. To achieve this 'liberation' all forms of fascism present themselves as a form of socialism; the socialist image, however, is always undermined by the nature of the racial or statist totality being offered. For at the heart of fascism is not the material emancipation of the working class but the taming of the masses.[12]

Fascism accepts one of Marx's insights into the nature of capitalism: by being the class with a material investment in the overthrow of capitalism, the working class constitutes *the* revolutionary threat to capitalism. Fascism mobilizes this revolutionary energy while simultaneously taming the force behind it. As Walter Benjamin puts it:

> Fascism attempts to organize the newly created proletarian masses without affecting the property structure which the masses strive to eliminate. Fascism sees its salvation in giving these masses not their right, but instead a chance to express themselves. The masses have a right to change property relations; fascism seeks to give them an expression while preserving property.[13]

To the extent that fascism tames the working class it reveals itself as a mechanism in the service of the capitalist order. To get to grips with the phenomenon of fascism, then, we must grasp its integral relationship with capitalism. This highlights the importance of Max Horkheimer's claim that 'whoever is not willing to talk about capitalism should also keep quiet about fascism'. Horkheimer's comment is helpful but, as Tim Mason points out, it does not tell us exactly *what* we have to say about the relationship.[14] That we do have to talk about capitalism if we are to talk about fascism will become clear. My concern in what follows is not with 'big business and the rise of Hitler and Mussolini', however; nor am I concerned with the so-called logic of monopoly capitalism.[15] Instead I shall focus on the relationship between capitalism and fascism and the fact that, despite its self-designation as socialist and its appropriation of some of the language, slogans and liturgy of the left, fascism established itself historically as a defence of capitalism and thus a *reaction* against working-class revolutionary potential. This will show that the film-maker Sergei Eisenstein's description of 'national socialism' as a 'mongrel of lies' is an apt description of all fascist 'socialism'.[16]

Fascism sits comfortably in the tradition of reactionary thought which identifies money and finance capital rather than capitalist commodity production as the 'enemy'. The goal in this tradition is not a classless society and the abolition of exploitation but a 'people's community' in which the excesses of the money-based modern society are curbed. Fascist attacks on 'capital' are always attacks on finance or banking capital rather than capitalist production. Despite operating under the label 'socialist', such attacks are always the hallmark of pseudo-socialist movements, that is, movements which steer clear of tackling the foundations of capitalist society. (It is precisely this kind of socialism which Marx and Engels attack in *The Communist Manifesto*.) Those who attack finance and banking capital play into the hands of industrial capital. Far from being anti-capitalist, fascism's attack on finance, banking and money capital constitutes a capitulation to fascist capitalist production.[17] Admittedly, distinguishing between 'creative' and 'parasitic' capital appeals to workers – by creating a mystique of socialist intentions – but, crucially, in its attack on 'parasitical' banking or finance capital this distinction also appeals to capitalists. Thus, far from being established in opposition to private property, fascism establishes itself as private property's saviour. Mussolini made the point that as far as economics went he was a Manchester liberal, Hitler never tired of stating that one of the symptoms of decay was the slow disappearance of the right of private property, and the policy of the Parti Populaire Française was for profit to remain the motor of production, even in 'fascist socialism'.

Historically this meant that fascism faced the problem of defending private property while retaining a 'socialist' façade and mobilizing the masses behind it. The practical outcome of this was to defend private property against the working class by either eliminating workers' organizations or turning them into instruments for the furtherance of national unity. In both Italy and Germany the result was the institutional emasculation of the working-class movement. Interestingly, however, the institutional process had different conceptual underpinnings. In the Italian case, with its focus on the state as the unifying mechanism behind the nation and the juridical orientation this entailed, the institutional thrust took a corporate form. In Germany, by contrast, the emphasis on the organic *Volk* meant that the institutional thrust took the form of organizing – in the sense of *making organic* – labour and capital into a unity.

The corporate state in Italy provided the foundation for the incorporation of capital and labour. Intended as a third way between liberalism and communism, Italian corporatism sought to unify the nation by invoking the image of unity gleaned from medieval corporations. Instead of workers and capitalists on opposite sides of the class divide, all were to be thought of as 'producers' contributing to the success of the nation.[18] For this reason organizations with only workers' interests were replaced by those obeying the demand for fascist national unity. The socialist General Confederation of Labour was abolished, to be replaced by the Fascist Labour Confederation, given an extra stamp of approval with the Vidoni Pact of October 1925 in which the Confederation and the industrialists' Confederazione Generale dell'Industria Italiana (CGII) officially recognized each other as representatives of labour and capital, respectively. Labour legislation the following year officially recognized one labour and one capital organization for each of the major branches of economic activity. In 1928 the fascist union structure was broken up into six smaller and weaker federations, overseen by the Ministry of Corporations. Finally, in 1934 an attempt was made to bring about a fully corporate order by dividing the economy into three large sectors – industry, agriculture and services – and within this the establishment of a system of 22 corporations. By 1938 these had been given representation in a newly created Chamber of Fasces and Corporations which replaced the Chamber of Deputies.

Debates over the extent to which Italy had a 'fully' corporate economy tend to miss the point of these historical developments. Like all attempts at the corporate organization of capitalist society, the purpose of fascist corporations was, on the surface,

> that of correcting and neutralizing a condition brought about by the industrial revolution of the nineteenth century which dissociated capital and labour in industry, giving rise on the one hand to a capitalist class of employers of labour and on the other to a great propertyless class, the industrial proletariat.[19]

In other words, to settle disputes between labour and capital, on opposite sides of the class divide. But while organized capital continued to be represented by its own spokesmen in the CGII, labour found itself 'represented' by fascist party bureaucrats, as formalized by the Vidoni agreement (and usefully assisted by the fact that the original leaders and representatives of labour were either in prison or underground). The juridical form appeared to overcome the traditional confrontation between capital and labour in the formerly 'private' sphere, but whereas capital still had a great deal of autonomy and freedom, labour was a subjugated force. The CGII was 'nominally subject to the same government controls that applied to other syndical associations but, unlike them, it was strong enough to resist the demands of government officials and Fascist radicals'.[20] Organized industry was *in* the state but not *of* the state; organized labour, on the other hand, was 'free' only to the extent that it was *of* the state. A corporate system forms a mystified veil behind which the process of capital accumulation continues un-hindered. By incorporating the working class, fascism nullifies the potential political action of that class and, in turn, facilitates the extraction of surplus value.

Two features of the Nazis' anti-capitalist rhetoric are important. First, the Nazi attack on unproductive or finance capital was equally an attack on Jewish capital. And, second, the Nazis also consist-ently attacked communism, Marxism, and demands for workers' autonomy and the heightening of the class struggle. These two features were combined in Nazi ideology through the insistence that there existed a Jewish–Bolshevik world conspiracy which was simultaneously a mechanism for the domination of finance capital-ism. The Nazis presented themselves as the saviours of socialism through their fight against Jewish–Bolshevik domination. Goebbels was to declare that 'socialism can be achieved only in opposition to the Jews, and it is because we want socialism that we are anti-Semitic', and in *Mein Kampf* Hitler openly professed that the Jew, like the Marxist, encourages contempt for the worker and seeks to shatter the national economy.[21] Yet the equation of 'capitalism' with 'Jewish capitalism' also facilitates the ideological substitution of race for class as the collective basis for struggle. The resulting 'socialism of the stupid', as August Bebel described anti-Semitism, required the composing of new words such as *jüdischer Finanzbolschewismus* to capture the combination of Jew, capitalist and communist collective enemy.[22]

The Nazis began by encouraging the trade unions to dissolve their links with the Social Democratic Party, winning the unions over by declaring 1 May a national holiday – a 'Day of National Labour'. In front of some 1 million people, in a celebration of the 'communal workers' state' and in honour of the 'productive workers of all classes', Hitler spoke out against the Marxist misunderstanding of manual labour and its presentation of society as torn apart by social class conflict. Like the Jew, the Marxist is said to denigrate manual labour. The Nazis, in contrast, would praise the work and industry of the people and end the isolation of classes and ranks. The following day, independent trade unionism was crushed. Neumann aptly summarizes the process:

> On 1 May 1933, the new national holiday was celebrated. A number of trade-union officials and a few members, still hoping to save their organizational structure, participated side by side with the National Socialists. The next day truck-loads of Brown Shirts and Black Shirts raided all union headquarters, arrested the leaders, seized the funds, and placed National Socialists in charge . . . It took exactly thirty minutes for the huge trade-union structure to collapse.[23]

In fact the breaking of the trade unions was more complex than this. Following Hitler's thoughts on trade unions in *Mein Kampf*, where he had argued that the problem was the *Marxist* use of trade unions to foment class divisions and thus undermine national unity rather than trade unions themselves, the Nazi regime smashed trade unions thought to be under the control of communists or containing workers who were communist sympathizers; other unions continued to exist after 1933.[24]

Initially the Nazis looked to the Italian corporate state as a possible model – in May 1933 the National Socialist Institute for Corporatism was established and major economists were arguing that corporatism was consistent with national socialism.[25] But the corporative set-up was abandoned because, by incorporating workers and employers into distinct bodies, the corporate form implied that these bodies were somehow separate. This contradicted the Nazi insistence on national homogeneity. In fact, the Nazis had to hand a set of categories with which they could resolve the worker problem without resorting to the juridical and statist form used in Italian fascism. That was the biological *Volk* community which by virtue of its form could be a solution to both the worker problem and the Jewish question simultaneously. This was developed at both national level and at the level of the firm.

On a national level the German Labour Front was established to end the divisions brought about by work specialization. The working class was first atomized and then reclassified according to 16 federal plant communities. But the individual workers were members not of one of the communities but of the total organization – the Labour Front – an organization for all working men, irrespective of their economic or social standing. The Labour Front was an organization of the totality of German people, without distinction as to class, occupation or social status. The Front was the institutionalized form of the doctrine that classes – and thus class conflict – no longer existed.

At the level of the firm one of the earliest pieces of legislation seeking a solution to the 'problem' of the working class was the Law on the Organization of National Labour (*Arbeitsordnungsgesetz*, or AOG). All institutions previously concerned with labour relations – from mass organizations to arbitration authorities – were to be replaced by the 'factory community' (*Betriebsgemeinschaft*) which, in turn, was to be the 'cell' of the national community (*Volksgemeinschaft*), a model of society which Hitler described as a 'process of coming together' of the 'artificial classes' in the nation. The employer as head of the workforce was to be the mirror image of a *Führer*; workers, to be known as his 'followers', were to swear 'fealty and obedience' to him, while he was to be concerned with the welfare of his workers. This would help develop the workers' inner commitment to the firm, loyalty to the leader, integration in the factory community and thus into the national community. Although the Trustees of Labour (from May 1933) stood above the 'community of the firm' to protect the interests of the state, such protection meant as little interference as possible as the responsibility for day-to-day problems was to remain with the cells of the social organism. A new system of 'social honour courts' was introduced in which 'offences against social honour' would be punished. Such offences included an employer overexploiting his workforce and a worker threatening the industrial peace.[26] The effects of these changes are obvious: emasculate the working-class movement by obliterating its institutional basis while simultaneously increasing the authority and power of the factory 'leaders' to dominate the workforce.

This domination operated alongside both the more overt repression of the workers and their representatives – the presence of the Gestapo at strikes and, from 1938, its terroristic surveillance over workers, including the use of miniature concentration camps attached to major industrial firms (of which there were 165 up to the middle of the war) – and the appropriation of the language and iconography of socialism. Not content with crushing the working-class movement, torturing and killing socialists, fascism also steals the jewellery from the corpse: the colour red, the street, the flag, May Day, socialist film-making, all adopted for the ideology of the nation and state power rather than world revolution.[27]

The different practices of the Italian and German fascist regimes are, on the one hand, a reflection of their very different ideological mechanisms for the subsumption of class struggle: in the Italian case the incorporation of the working class through a juridical and statist corporate form, in the German case through the organization of the factory as a community, in turn being the cell of the national community. Mussolini and Gentile's claim that there must be nothing outside the state is as much a *legal* as it is philosophical or political conception. To the extent that this applies to corporations it points to the fact that corporatism rests on the *juridical* recognition of the professional associations *as* corporations ('professional' here being the fascist term which includes both workers' and employers' unions). Associations can only be corporations if constituted as such by the state. The Nazis rejected such juridical forms, believing that the statist and legalistic orientation of corporatism smacked of the systematic institutionalization and juridification of social differences. Instead of corporatism the Nazis, with their adherence to more biologistic forms of thought, set about *organizing* the economy and social life. By this I mean not the planning of the economy, but the creation of an *organic form* for the units of economic life – factories, production plants, and so on. Instead of legal incorporation the Nazis 'organized' – that is, *organicized* – everything. The call for the creation of a 'biology of the firm' by leading economists, the publicity of the German Labour Front maintaining that it had grown organically and the passing of a Law for the Organic Construction of the German Economy are but three examples. Those features of economic and social life which were fundamental to the health of the nation – which eventually came to mean everything from factories to leisure clubs – had to be given an organic form so that it could be part of the higher organism of the nation.[28] 'Nature' was thus invoked as a solution to political and social problems.

On the other hand, these divergent ideological mechanisms possess an underlying unity of a twofold kind. First, the grounds for the taming of the working class were the presupposition of the necessity for national unity over class conflict. The different means for achieving this – incorporation or obliteration through organization

– rested none the less on the unity of the nation and authoritarian state power. What fascism understands by 'unity', then, is a nation-state in which oppressing and oppressed classes are forced together under a structure of domination.[29] 'Unity' here refers less to harmony than to class and state domination, with all forms of resistance and opposition effectively crushed. Second, these divergent mechanisms had a common core – a return to a mythic past, in which such unity was present. Italian corporations were an attempt to invoke the unity achieved by the medieval corporations, a revival of medieval form stuffed full of modern content (capitalism), and the organic form for factory communities in Germany was an attempt to redeem the lost unity of the medieval world. Both were reactions to modernity and its core political components of Marxism and liberalism, with their insistence that bourgeois society is divided on class lines or is merely a collection of atomized individuals. This last point is developed in the next chapter.

This 'resolution' of the class struggle had as its corollary an ideological commitment to work and the 'dignity' of labour; at its extreme this was a celebration of work as a liberating experience and thus one which could unite the nation. Capitalism's treatment of labour as a commodity, and Marxism's treatment of the worker as a proletarian, are interpreted by fascism as a sign that neither capitalism nor Marxism respects the real value of work. Fascism conceives itself as restoring the dignity of labour by overcoming the negative experience of it in both capitalism and communism. But through the refusal to abolish capitalism, the solution to alienation and exploitation has to assume an ideological form: the aestheticization of the workplace and the beautification of the everyday. In Nazi Germany, for example, this took the form of the 'Bureau of Beauty of Labour', founded in November 1933 as a branch of the leisure organization 'Strength through Joy', and its campaigns for various improvements to the workplace. Initially these were often purely technical, as in the 'Good Light – Good Work', 'Hot Food in the Plant' and 'Clean People in Clean Plants' campaigns, with the last of these resulting in widespread renovations of washing and wardrobe facilities. But they became increasingly aesthetic in their orientation. By insisting that the basis for joy in work and genuine satisfaction is only created by having work removed from the sphere of material considerations and given a higher, ethical meaning, the Bureau made beauty and joy the rhetorical organizing principles of industrial society.[30] To this end, new designs for the interiors of offices and factories were developed, including new designs for furniture, light fixtures and other interior furnishings. Plant leaders were encouraged to employ artists to brighten the workplace with wall mosaics. Lest the plant's capacity for capital accumulation be affected the Bureau was given advisory powers only; it lacked any legal authority to impose changes on the factory leader, and had no power to make unsolicited visits to factories. Moreover, one of the overall thrusts of the Beauty of Labour was to emphasize the economic return which the aestheticization of the workplace could bring through the increased performance of the worker. In the wider context of the ideology of the factory community and its leaders, and the demolition of autonomous working-class organizations, the Beauty of Labour was clearly a contribution to the ideology of capitalist enterprise. Hitler nevertheless referred to Beauty of Labour as the 'socialism of the deed'. It was 'socialist' because, as Anson Rabinbach notes, 'the historical experience of the proletariat was to be dissolved in the plant and national community'. With the Beauty of Labour, labour was deproletarianized and domesticated, turned into a beautiful activity far removed from the grubby world of work portrayed in Marxist and Jewish writings.[31] In other words, fascism redefines the problem of the worker as a psychological one and seeks to administer it politically.

The effect of these changes was to encourage capital accumulation, so long as capital would adapt to the regime. Illustrative here is Coca-Cola. By 1939 the soft drinks company had 43 bottling plants in Germany – sales had reached 4½ million cases – with nine more plants under construction. Each of these plants was modelled on the leadership principle, partly of necessity – to remain within the law – but also because the plants could then make use of low-waged and powerless workers. In more general terms, Coca-Cola had to dissociate itself from its American roots and international appeal, presenting itself as an authentically German product. It removed bottle caps reminding consumers that the drink was a kosher product, and it appeared in force at the 1936 Olympics in Berlin and numerous other sporting events advertised as a healthy drink suitable for German athletes. More, its trucks accompanied the Hitler Youth on their marches and the firm was happy to assist the Nazi propaganda machine while in pursuit of its own profits: in the Nazis' 1937 'Working People Exhibition' a functioning mini-bottling plant was at the heart of the fair, next to the Propaganda Office, while at its own concessionaire conferences its company banners nestled comfortably alongside swastikas. When Nazi troops marched into Austria in March 1938, Coca-Cola marched in right behind them, establishing a Vienna branch in September of that year.[32]

To the extent that fascism facilitates capital accumulation and crushes workers' organizations it reveals itself, regardless of its revolutionary rhetoric, as an essentially conservative political phenomenon in defence of capitalism, a political attempt to revive flagging capitalist economies by overcoming the political weaknesses of liberal democratic regimes. Fascism thus reveals the truth of capitalism. The meaning of this statement should not be misconstrued. I repeat my earlier point: I am making no specific claims about the financing of fascist parties and regimes by German and Italian big business; nor am I suggesting that fascism is in some way the logic of monopoly capitalism. Inter-war fascism was no more an expression of monopoly capital than the New Deal or Weimar itself.[33] Industrial capital can come to terms with any political regime so long as that regime does not actually expropriate it, and will willingly and happily come to terms with any regime which solves economic depression, ends political chaos, destroys the revolutionary communist and socialist movement, eliminates workers' institutions, and commits itself to industrial (capitalist) modernization. Attempts to describe fascism under categories such as totalitarianism, state capitalism and bureaucratic collectivism fail to address this; indeed, they mask it over. Horkheimer's comment, that whoever is not willing to talk about capitalism should also keep quiet about fascism, is thus well made, despite arguments to the contrary made by historians of the opposite political persuasion.[34] But if fascism reveals the truth of capitalism, its defence of capitalism also reveals the truth of fascism.

One of the reasons why this issue has been downplayed in some of the recent literature on fascism is the primacy of politics found in fascist theory and practice. For fascism, the crucial feature of modern order is the political, the very sphere which Marxists and liberals are said to denigrate. For fascism, Marxism treats the political as an epiphenomenon of the economic, while liberalism treats it as mere night-watchman, overseeing a self-regulating civil society. The fascist response is to emphasize the political over the economic, to work, in effect, with a strong concept of the political, collapsing the state–civil society distinction and subsuming civil society under the state – nothing outside of the state. The ideological effect of this is that fascism works without an economic doctrine to speak of. The practical effect is a fairly *laissez-faire* attitude to capital accumulation. Its solution to the economic contradictions and crises of capitalism is ever more authoritarian state power. For this reason commentators have tended to focus their analyses here, on the political. But the stress on the primacy of politics obscures the continuation of structures of *social* domination.

But then what of fascism's own insistence that it constitutes a revolutionary political doctrine and the widespread desire to take fascism at its own word on this issue? Broadly speaking, there are two ways in which fascism has been interpreted as a revolutionary doctrine. The first concerns its orientation to capitalism, and the second a more general question of its orientation to modernity. Discussion of the second of these will be left to the next chapter. The remainder of this chapter lays the groundwork for the argument by further developing the claim that the defence of capitalism reveals the truth of fascism. Part of this discussion will necessarily involve an account of the concept of revolution, for in many ways it is with this concept that the misunderstanding arises, a misunderstanding that can be overcome by recognizing fascism as the culmination of a conservative revolutionary tradition.

The politics of revolution

Moeller van den Bruck once described the German revolution of 1918 as 'a revolution with no enthusiasm'. What was lacking was the collective national spirit of 1914. Hence Moeller began *The Third Reich* in 1922 by insisting on the need for a successful revolution, that is, a revolution by those who would not stab the army in the back, give in to Germany's enemies and turn their backs on German values and culture.[35] The revolution, then, would not be a socialist one. Rather than a transformation of the material conditions of exploitation and the structures of social domination, the revolution would be in German culture, an essentially spiritual revolution for the nation.

Moeller here provides the key to understanding the fascist insistence that it is revolutionary. Fascism undoubtedly does present itself as a revolutionary doctrine and its seizure of power as a revolution. Mussolini and Gentile continually insisted that fascism was revolutionary,[36] and leading Nazis referred to their movement as revolutionary and the regime itself as constituting a national or national socialist revolution.[37] Many commentators have taken these claims at face value and, by pointing to the supposedly revolutionary changes that the fascist regimes brought about, take the fascist claim one step further. First mooted by Hermann Rauschning in his description of Nazism as a 'revolution of nihilism', the claim has been extended to incorporate arguments that Hitler did achieve a genuine social revolution or that the revolution was one of destruction, paving the way for the modernization of German society. Similar claims are made for Italy.[38] In whatever shape they come, such claims are generally intended as a riposte to Marxist arguments that fascism is by definition a counter-revolutionary and reactionary movement.

One of the difficulties faced by anyone dealing with the question of the 'revolutionary' nature of fascism is that they enter what has been called a 'semantic minefield',[39] with associated concepts such as 'counter-revolutionary' and 'reactionary' only adding to the dangers. The minefield is made more hazardous by fascist ideology itself: as much as the fascists present themselves as revolutionary, and may sincerely think of themselves as such, they also think of themselves as counter-revolutionary and reactionary. Mussolini describes fascism in *any* language he finds useful. In regarding itself as somehow beyond all intellectual systems fascism freely borrows from them all; by being anti-systematic and anti-intellectual it does not matter whether this borrowing renders fascism unintelligible. The fact that fascism is, for Mussolini, some kind of glorious synthesis of opposites means that fascists can be 'aristocrats and democrats, revolutionaries and reactionaries, proletarians and anti-proletarians, pacifists and anti-pacifists'.[40] Hitler notoriously declared himself a revolutionary against the revolution.

One of the reasons why so many have lost intellectual limbs in this minefield is the careless use of the concept of revolution and, where it is not being used carelessly, the widely divergent meanings attached to the word: in some cases it refers to the demands made in fascist ideology, in others it refers to the seizure of power, while in yet others it is taken to refer to a social revolution said to have occurred in Italy and Germany once power had been seized. The confusion here is one handed down to us by the English and French revolutions (and, to a lesser extent, the Bolshevik one). But the confusion does not require us to jettison the concept of revolution (and, relatedly, counter-revolution) as some suggest.[41] One way to use the concept of revolution is to distinguish between political and social revolution, where the former represents a transformation of political power relations and the latter a transformation in the socio-economic relations of production. Revolution can be thought of as both process and moment, where a process of revolutionary social transformation is accompanied by moments of revolutionary political change. This is the kind of distinction Marx operates with. Although for Marx 1640 and 1789 are revolutionary *moments*, the general thrust of his concern is the long term *process* by which capitalist relations of production come to dominate. It is for this reason that he points to an 'era of social revolution'. The strength of this lies in being able to distinguish between the long, slow and often 'silent' process by which a particular mode of production and its concomitant property relations place their stamp on human relations, and the moments of political rupture or crisis in which relations of political power and authority undergo substantial alteration. As Geoff Eley puts it in his account of the 'peculiarities' of German history:

> Abstractly this means distinguishing between two levels of determination and significance – between the revolution as a specific crisis of the state, involving widespread popular mobilization and a reconstitution of political relationships, and on the other hand the deeper processes of structural change, involving the increasing predominance of the capitalist mode of production.[43]

Crucially, revolutionary political moments need not necessarily contribute to a longer process of social revolution.

Clearly the seizures of power by the fascists in both Germany and Italy were reactions to the perceived crises of the state and threat of communist revolution. In Germany the failure of the political elites and institutions of the Weimar Republic to overcome the economic crises created an opening for an authoritarian intervention. In providing this intervention the Nazis obliterated the Weimar constitution and thus liberal democracy in Germany. Whether this constituted a *political* revolution is at least questionable: the old political elites continued to exist alongside the new Nazi elites, and key institutions such as the civil service and the army retained a large degree of autonomy.[44] That it did not constitute a *social* revolution is clear: the class structure remained more or less intact. In the case of Italy one may wish to describe the seizure of power as a revolutionary political moment, but thereafter the regime had no long-term revolutionary effect on the nature of the social structure. The fascist regime emerged as a new authoritarian political defence of the increasingly capitalist social order. As a centralized and authoritarian regime it could carry out some degree of social transformation – it managed to usurp Mafia power bases, for example – but at no point sought to undermine the real class structure then in existence.[45]

If we concede that the fascist seizure of power constituted a revolutionary form of government in that the political institutions and processes of liberal democracy were obliterated in both Germany and Italy, we must nevertheless also argue that both regimes failed to produce a revolutionary transformation of social power. It is for this reason that the Nazis saw the seizure of political power as the completion of the revolution (Hitler) or the last stage of a revolutionary act (Goebbels), and that as early as 1924 Mussolini was describing the fascist 'revolution' as at an end; Mussolini also pointed to all the things it had *not* done, that is, all the things the fascist 'revolution' had in fact preserved.[46]

Fascism sets itself against the possibility of a communist – that is, social – revolution. The fascist political revolution is the *alternative* to social revolution; as such it is equally counter-revolutionary.[47] Hitler's description of himself as a revolutionary against the revolution thus reveals much about fascism. The double meaning of the description – on the one hand it was a revolution against the revolution of 1918 (and thus also the October revolution of the previous year), and on the other hand it was a revolution to block any future communist revolution – reveals that the fascist revolution has an essentially conservative nature. It is for this reason that liberal democracies were happy with the fascist regimes. (For example, in 1937 Lord Halifax told Hitler that he and other government colleagues 'were fully aware that the Führer had not only achieved a great deal inside Germany herself, but that, by destroying communism in his country, he had barred its road to

Western Europe and that Germany therefore could rightly be regarded as a bulwark of the West against Bolshevism'.[48]) Fascism's politically revolutionary effect – the imposition of an authoritarian regime as an illiberal solution to crises – reveals its socially conservative and counter-revolutionary essence. For this reason we can describe fascism as the culmination of the *conservative revolutionary* tradition.

Ideas concerning a conservative revolution emerged during the 1920s among radical right groups, especially, though not exclusively, in Germany. Popularized by Hugo von Hofmannsthal's attempt in 1927 to capture what he thought was an increasingly powerful political movement to create a spiritual unity out of a fragmented social order, conservative revolution was considered as both a counter-movement to the general 'spiritual upheaval' of the nineteenth century – essentially, the idea of Enlightenment and its rationalist political projects – and, more particularly, a means of articulating radical nationalist demands – that is, an argument for the reassertion of the nation and national pride via a strengthening of state power against the competing groups and social forces within civil society.[49] As one writer put it:

> By 'conservative revolution' we mean the return to respect for all those elementary laws and values without which the individual is alienated from nature and God . . . In the place of equality comes the inner value of the individual; in the place of socialist convictions, the just integration of people into their place in a society of rank; in place of mechanical selection, the organic growth of leadership; in place of bureaucratic compulsion, the inner responsibility of genuine self-governance; in place of mass happiness, the rights of the personality formed by the nation.[50]

It is clear that the conservative revolutionaries – including Moeller, Hofmannsthal, Edgar Jung, Ernst Jünger, Carl Schmitt and Hans Freyer – formed the intellectual vanguard of the right in Germany and as such provided intellectual justification for the undermining of Weimar democracy. Fascism appropriated the central themes articulated by the conservative revolutionaries, radicalized them and put them into practice. And this applies to fascism generally: even before the march on Rome, Mussolini was claiming that one could be both revolutionary and conservative.[51]

This reading of fascism – to be developed further in the next chapter – undermines the attempt to present it as a 'third way' between capitalism and communism or as 'neither right nor left'. Supposedly the synthesis of all oppositions, fascism freely claims that it also overcomes the artificial right–left distinction. The Spanish fascist, José Antonio Primo de Rivera, sums up the position: fascism is neither right nor left because

> basically the Right stands for the maintenance of an economic structure, albeit an unjust one, while the Left stands for the attempt to subvert that economic structure, even though the subversion thereof would entail the destruction of much that was worthwhile.[52]

If 'the right' is associated with the defence of private property then fascism, given its supposed ideological opposition to capitalism, has to declare itself to be not of the right. But because of the integral links between Marxism, revolutionary anti-capitalism and 'the left', fascism also has to differentiate itself from the left generally. This leaves fascism in an apparent no man's land in the battleground of political thought, which it reinterprets positively as the transcendence of false dichotomies. But the fact that fascism's opposition to capitalism is an attack on parasitical finance capital but not capitalism *per se* means that fascism is never a third way between capitalism and communism, whatever its own ideologues might say. Even those commentators who take seriously fascist claims to be a third way recognize this to be the case. George Mosse, for example, after an insightful account of the differences in third way arguments across the continent, concedes in the end that while fascism sought a third way between capitalism and Marxism, it also sought to 'escape concrete economic and social change by a retreat into ideology'. Likewise Zeev Sternhell, despite suggesting that 'it is misleading to identify fascism with the right', nevertheless concedes that 'in practice . . . fascism's insistence on the cooperation of all social classes and their reconciliation within the corporative regime threw it irrevocably to the right'.[53]

Moreover, fascists know full well that their enemy is on the left: it is, after all, left-wing and not right-wing activists who fill the cells of fascist prisons. Conservative elites may be boring, flabby, impotent and decrepit, but they do not constitute the same kind of danger to fascism as socialism and communism. If fascism is revolutionary, then, it is a particular form of conservative revolution, and thus a revolution from the right.

Revolution against the Revolution II: Fascism as Reactionary Modernism

What does it mean to speak of a revolution from the right? Is it not oxymoronic to speak of conservative revolution? Some commentators have argued that fascism is revolutionary not because of its commitment to capitalism *per se*, but because of its orientation to modernity in general. Ralf Dahrendorf, for example, describes Nazism as a 'break with tradition' and thus 'a strong push toward modernity', despite the Nazi leaders' self-professed love of traditional rural life and hatred of modernity. Nazism, on this account, played a crucial role in the modernizing process in Germany.[1] A. James Gregor has likewise argued that fascism was a crucial episode in the modernization of Italy. Against this some have argued that fascism's reactionary moment is best captured in its desire for a return to a traditional order and mythic past. Hans Rogger argues that 'in the final reckoning . . . the Right represents not the wave of the future but a nihilistic hostility to modernity', while George Mosse insists that Nazism in particular formed a 'general opposition to modernity'. Such accounts tally with Fritz Stern's argument that the politics of cultural despair which gave rise to Nazism had its roots in a negative reaction to modernity.[2] Within this debate the issue of a generic fascism again rears its head, for some have argued that the difference between Italian fascism and Nazism is best captured through their incompatible approaches to modernity and tradition: whereas Nazism is a backward looking and thus essentially reactionary phenomenon, fascism 'proper' is said to be oriented towards the future and thus accepts the essential nature of modernity. Renzo de Felice, Michael Leeden and others claim that whereas Nazism sought to liberate the true Aryan of the past from his suffocation by the strictures of modernity, in the process making Nazism an anti-modern force, Italian fascism wanted instead to create a new man, and this gave Italian fascism a very different orientation to modernity.[3]

I shall cut across these claims by arguing that fascism is a form of *reactionary modernism*, a term I am adopting from Jeffrey Herf's work on technology and culture in the Weimar Republic and the Third Reich.[4] Expressing a commitment to *both* modernity *and* a mythicized past, fascism is both modern and reactionary, and it is as a form of reactionary modernism that fascism reveals its role as the culmination of the conservative revolution.

One can think of reactionary modernism as *modernist* in two ways. First, as technological modernization: reactionary modernists express a love of technological development, as a means of developing the economically productive capabilities of the nation, but also for technology's own sake. This is expressed in the love of new technological forms of transport and communication – cars, aeroplanes and trains, radios and television. Second, it is modernist in its articulation of themes found in the work of writers central to the modernist vanguard such as Ernst Jünger and Gottfried Benn in Germany, Marinetti and the futurists in Italy, Ezra Pound and Wyndham Lewis in England: the freeing of the creative spirit, the triumph of the will over reason, the transcending of the restricting, stifling and boring world of the bourgeois, a fascination for horror and violence, the glorification of commitment and engagement in the search for the authentic self.

One problem is immediately encountered in talking about the modern, however. Current thinking about modernity is broken up into different compartments, which appear hermetically sealed off from one another: 'modernization' often refers to technological advancement, especially in the economic realm; 'modern' is frequently taken to be a politico-historical referent; 'modernism' refers to forms of artistic and cultural production.[5] Nevertheless, we can say that in each case the modern is contrasted with the traditional and backward-looking: economic growth within an increasingly industrialized system is paradigmatically opposed to attitudes and structures seen as obstructive and irrational; new modes of thought, means of expression and innovative cultural practices are paradigmatically opposed to traditional forms of cultural production. Much of the current literature on fascism, however, tends to oscillate blindly between these 'compartments'. Not only does this add to the problematic fuzziness the term has, it also acts as an obstacle in the attempt to develop a critical account of the relationship between fascism and modernity.

Here the essential connection between fascism and capitalism made in the previous chapter is important, for capitalism is widely recognized as *the* socio-economic system of modernity. As the key determining feature of a society, capitalism shapes that society in its own image, perpetually transforming social relations in the pursuit of the maximization of profit. This has a seriously dislocating effect on those who live these social relations. As Marx and Engels write:

> Constant revolutionizing of production, uninterrupted disturbance of all social conditions, everlasting uncertainty and agitation distinguish the bourgeois epoch from all earlier ones. All fixed, fast-frozen relations, with their train of ancient and venerable prejudices and opinions are swept away, all new-formed ones become antiquated before they can ossify. All that is solid melts into air, all that is holy is profaned, and man is at last compelled to face with sober senses, his real conditions of life, and his relations with his kind.[6]

Markets which are static collapse under the weight of inertia; stability means entropy. The *social* effects of this are drastic: the imperative to innovate and change produces continued social dislocation and disruption, everlasting uncertainty and agitation. We shall return to this point.

One can think of reactionary modernism as *reactionary* because it is clearly a movement of the political right: reactionary modernism opposes the principles of 1789 adopted by liberals and given a critical edge by socialists, and finds in nationalism a force supposedly 'beyond' Marxism and capitalism. Adopting conservative revolutionary arguments, reactionary modernism establishes as its guide for action a set of social forms which no longer exist, and perhaps never did, but which assume a mythic status and form the basis of emotional investment on a mass scale. These social forms are often based on presuppositions concerning a *natural* or *national* essence.

Fascism and modernity

The momentous transformation in the understanding of the culture of time and space brought about by the revolt against positivism was partly a result of the effect of new forms of technology which appeared to be reshaping the nature of society. The telephone, wireless, photography, cinema, automobile, airplane and X-ray together constituted a transformation in commonly held views concerning time and space. The telephone, for example, not only made communication so much faster, but also appeared to allow the user to be in two places at one time. The destructive effects of this transformation were brought home on the battlefields of the First World War.[7]

The new speed of time and the breakdown of traditional spatial forms were reflected in artistic movements such as cubism and futurism, of which the latter saw itself as a directly political as well as artistic movement. The political links between Italian futurists and fascism are well established – F.T. Marinetti participated in the burning of the offices of the socialist paper *Avanti* in 1919 and was appointed to the *Accademia d'Italia* in 1929 – but it is the theoretical contours and presuppositions of the movement that are important here. As early as the 1909 publication of 'The Founding and Manifesto of Futurism', the futurists made clear the political directions of the movement. Adopting Nietzschean, Sorelian and Bergsonian language and motifs, the praise the futurists heaped on the glory of war 'as the world's greatest hygiene' was based on the status accorded to speed, destruction and violence against the bourgeois order. The object was to usher in a new order based on Italian national glory. This break with the recent past would be achieved through aestheticizing the everyday by reifying and radicalizing its supposedly natural form – struggle, violence and speed.[8]

This aesthetics of speed and struggle simultaneously forms the basis of a new morality and promotes *technology* as the form through which this new morality is to be expressed. As the highpoint of the new religion of speed, technology gives expression to the new human praxis, an 'inevitable identification of man with motor' which aestheticizes technology and power. It is in this conception of technology that fascism and futurism meet. Far from learning from the futurists only a certain technique of invective, a means of popular agitation and the value of destroying bourgeois values,[9] fascism adopted the futurist aestheticization of technology, speed and violence. Since fascism is a dynamo, anything remotely connected to dynamism undergoes a process of sanctification – new motorways, new means of transport (Fiat cars), new forms of communication (Olivetti typewriters), indeed any new mechanism for the technological mastery of nature. In other words, fascism expresses a commitment to modern technology, and it is partly this commitment which enabled the fascist modernization of Italy. Not only did the trains run on time, but the train became a living symbol of the new Italy – an electrified, technologically advanced and tightly interconnected industrial nation founded on the values of efficiency, speed, and technical innovation.[10]

When Marinetti visited Nazi Germany in the spring of 1934, he was greeted in the name of the National Socialist Writers' Union by Germany's most important poet, Gottfried Benn, who praised the futurists' love of danger and speed, fearlessness and stress on the nation.[11] The Nazis, of course, abhorred 'modern' art, but the links between artistic modernist movements were mirrored in the appropriation of technology and technological motifs, and the focus on speed, motion and innovation. 'We live', according to Goebbels, 'in an era of technology. The racing tempo of our century affects all areas of our life. There is scarcely an endeavour that can escape its powerful influence'.[12] As is well known, 'Hitler relished speeding through the countryside in his powerful Mercedes-Benz convertible or descending dramatically out of the clouds in a chartered airplane', and his private conversations reveal a fascination with technology.[13] Hitler was expressing part of the culture of technology and technological fetishism that dominated political and philosophical debates in general and reactionary modernist arguments in particular. In the work of conservative revolutionaries such as Ernst Jünger, for example, technology is conceived of as a manifestation of the will to power, which is in turn reconceived as technological domination structured through the nation; a nation oriented for war through technology results in total mobilization. Total mobilization has as its end not victory in war but the creation of a new race mobilized for war and for the use of technology as the means of planetary control. 'I see a new, leading race . . . which builds and defies machines, for whom machines are not dead iron, but organs of power which it governs with cold understanding and hot blood. This gives the world a new look'.[14] Nazism adopted such arguments, claiming that an anti-technology stance was a recipe for national impotence. To be strong in the twentieth century the nation has to be technologically advanced. Moreover, the distinction drawn between creative and parasitic capital is also assumed to rest on the subordination of technology to the wrong forces. Freed from domination by capitalist exchange and brought under political control, technology can be a liberating force.

This commitment to the speed and dynamism of modernity as the 'tempo of our century' is illustrated in the way language and symbols were used and manipulated. The insignia of the SS, for example, is now written with a double Roman S. But for the Nazis it was a symbol appropriated from Teutonic runes, *SS* . These two letters are *zackig*, a military term from the First World War best translated as 'jagged' and 'snappy', but also representing lightning. By using two of them together, in silver on a black background, the pictorial effect is to present the viewer with a dynamic visual, a symbol of regime in motion. The Nazis adopted their technology to this end – official typewriters were adapted to be able to produce the *SS* .[15] The swastika can be read in a similar fashion. In *The Sense of Order*, E.H. Gombrich points to the way the swastika lacks a mirror symmetry, of the kind we immediately look for in our visual environment. That the swastika has always been felt to be endowed with a certain dynamic energy comes from the fact that, given its lack of symmetry, we 'rotate' the swastika in an imaginary fashion in order to find some kind of symmetry. Because no symmetry can be found the rotation becomes perpetual. Reading the swastika as a symbol in and of perpetual motion – symbol of the perpetual motion of the movement in power, the forward march of Nazism into and through the modern world – highlights certain aspects of Leni Riefenstahl's film *Triumph of the Will* (1934). The opening sequence is of Hitler's aeroplane – the most technologically advanced form of transport – descending as it approaches Nuremburg. Its tailfin is adorned with the swastika. Here the conjunction is of the most advanced technology and the symbol of perpetual motion. And by turning the city into a sea of waving swastika banners the swastika became a symbol of total mobilization. The movement is complete: mass mobilization, technology, perpetual motion. Together they serve witness to the Nazis commitment to modernity.[16]

Fascism also utilizes and participates in the development of the most up-to-date and 'modern' mechanisms of production. In the 1920s and 1930s Taylorism, Fordism and scientific management – what became known as Americanism or the Americanist vision – appealed to fascism, offering highly technologized production with strict hierarchical divisions and new forms of management which nevertheless had the appearance of breaking with traditional work organizations. Taylorism appeared to offer capitalism without class: a new 'productivist' ideology rooted in technology rather than capital. This also gave the opportunity for talking about new forms of leadership. Instead of capitalists and managers the new productivist ideology talked of 'experts', subsuming questions of power into technical questions requiring experts. This allowed reactionary modernists such as Oswald Spengler to place the machine at the heart of modernity and to talk of the manager and the engineer as 'the priest of the machine'.[17]

Perhaps most significantly, nothing exemplifies the holocaust more than its essentially *modern* aspects. Far from being some kind of throw-back to pre-modern barbarism, the holocaust required modernity as one of its necessary conditions. As Zygmunt Bauman notes, there is more than a fortuitous connection between the applied technology of the production line and the applied technology of the concentration camp. The holocaust could not have occurred had the Nazis' treatment of Jews been restricted to events such as the pogrom of November 1938 (euphemistically known as *Kristallnacht*). For the mass slaughter of millions, and thus for the most *modern* form of barbarism, what was needed was the application of Taylorism and the principles of scientific management, on the one hand, and the most advanced technological processes on the other. As Bauman puts it, 'the story of the organization of the Holocaust could be made into a textbook of scientific management'.[18] Witch-hunts and other forms of barbarism were not needed to exorcise modern Europe's inner demons – modern science, technology and industrial processes could perform the task far more efficiently and rationally.

The past as future

It is clear, then, that far from engaging in an assault on modernity or processes central to modernity such as industrialization and technological advance, fascism embraces them. Yet it is none the less also the case that fascism glorifies a mythic past, is backward-looking and thus *anti-modern*, or so it would appear. Admittedly, this glorification of a mythic past may appear to be little more than the adoption of symbolic bric-à-brac culled from the remote past, as Arno Mayer puts it, but it is none the less central to fascist ideology and, perhaps, to the mass mobilization of support for fascism. Fascism colonizes the world of myth partly because communists and socialists frequently abandon it as part of the mystified realm of the irrational; yet in doing so fascism appropriates images and symbols which have populist appeal.[19]

Central to the myths cultivated by fascists in Italy was that of Rome and the cult of the *romanità*. Emilio Gentile claims that 'the myth of Rome was perhaps the most pervasive mythological belief in fascism's entire symbolic universe'.[20] For Mussolini 'Rome is our guiding star; it is our symbol – or, if you prefer, our myth'.[21] Here the fascist movement was given a boost by the seizure of Fiume by Gabriele d'Annunzio in September 1919. In the 15 months in which d'Annunzio held power in Fiume he developed what were to become characteristic forms of fascist style, appropriated from the myth of Rome. Having already invented the Roman salute for a 1914 film script, d'Annunzio dubbed his troops legionnaires after the Romans. The Italian fascists took this one step further. Fascism was to be led by a *Duce* (from the Latin *dux*), its symbol the *fasces* (the lictors' axe bound in rods) and its militia staffed with consuls, centurions and legionnaires. It incorporated key aspects of ancient Rome into the calendar, and its first public holiday was the 'Birth of Rome Day', to be celebrated as a fascist day of work in contrast to the class-oriented May Day. The March on Rome was compared with key Roman *coups d'état*. Roman symbolism such as the salute, the *passo romano* (the Italian version of the German goose-step), and Roman motifs in fascist architecture were all introduced.[22]

This appropriation of ancient Rome for the fascist movement was more than mere propaganda; it was also more than merely the fascist 'style' of politics. In Italy, Roman history was generally taken to be national Italian history. Fascism adopted and encouraged this view, propagating the cult of the *romanità* in numerous works of ideology. Aside from its crucial role in legitimizing fascist power, the cult of the *romanità* was also more generally designed to inculcate the virtues said to be required by a nation: law, order, justice, valour and dedication to collective interests. In contrast to the ancient Greeks and their mechanistic and individualistic understanding of state power and political order, the Romans had a conception of the state as a corporate entity under a strong leader. In other words, there existed a *virtus romana*, the quintessence of Roman-Italian history and civilization. The fascist spirit and thus the fascist regime were the realization of the virtues that had once made Italy (Rome) great.

The Nazis, of course, had no myth of ancient grandeur to invoke. Although the ancient Greeks were thought of as Aryan, allowing the Nazis to flirt with images from the ancient world – the dressing up of young girls in ancient garb at processions and festivals, for example – the mythic past for which the Nazis hankered was a medieval one, rooted in the desire for a return to traditional forms of unity rooted in the soil and based on essentially pre-modern forms of organization. This involved widespread use of Teutonic imagery: at the Day of German Art in Munich in 1939 the participants aped the German 'folk' tradition by dressing in medieval costume and carrying shields of knights.[23] But this was because the Nazis saw in the medieval world the basis for a unified social order, everything that was absent from the modern world. Crucial here is the attempt to invoke the feudal concepts of honour and loyalty as the basis of the natural political unit. In this sense the *Führerprinzip* was a twentieth-century reworking of the feudal principle of honour and loyalty. Likewise the Nazi doctrine of 'blood and soil' was based on its disdain for Roman law private property rights; what was needed was a more feudal notion of property based on the right of usufruct and inheritance in return for service rendered to the community. For these reasons the Nazis rejected modern notions of authority and obedience to rationally structured but anonymous state authority, replacing them instead with ties of personal loyalty, not only to the *Führer* but to a range of 'little Führers' via a series of subinfeudations conducted through oaths of loyalty. The medieval terminology here conceals the complete surrender of modern working-class rights. The working class had to be feudalized into a 'fealty' (*Gefolgschaft*), as a collection of feudally faithful noble Teutons – hence the importance of the factory community and its leader.[24]

As much as one can talk of fascist modernity, then, one must also recognize that this is simultaneously a form of *reaction*, an attempt to invoke nostalgic images in order to sustain state power and social order. Too much of the secondary literature on fascism has focused on the 'archaic' elements in fascism and has thus presented fascism as the politics of reaction in a manner which is anti-modern pure and simple. If we can speak about fascist modernism, however, then clearly we have identified as central to fascism what might appear to be contradictory forces – dynamism versus stability, innovation versus order, technological advance versus traditional structures – which in fact constitute the central tensions found in political thought on the right generally. This tension is played out in fascist theory and practice.

The Nazis' Beauty of Labour became the centre for the modernizing thrust of national socialism, but by combining this with feudal ideals the Beauty of Labour promoted what appears to be a uniquely fascist *synthesis* of modernity and anti-modernity. Its vision of a classless people's community based on honour and loyalty but which was none the less capable of competing with the major industrial powers epitomized the extent to which Nazism fused styles of industrial modernism with anti-modern motifs. Not only were industrial plants to have murals depicting pre-modern, rural, *völkisch* scenes painted inside them, but the Bureau also encouraged the redesign of the entrance and gate of the plant in wrought iron with medieval figures. The leisure organization Strength through Joy promoted modern high-speed ocean travel to palm-lined beaches and motorized outings through medieval landscapes, while the *Autobahn* project in Germany was deliberately planned to pass through areas of scenic beauty in order that they might appear to work in harmony with nature and the rural life; the same is true of motorways in fascist Italy. And the swastika, as much as it is a symbol of perpetual motion and total mobilization, is also a pre-modern symbol, a syncretic combination of the archaic within the modern.[25]

This syncretism is also revealed in the 1932 Exhibition of the Fascist Revolution in Italy. The exhibition was to commemorate not just the fascist revolution but also the revolution as a re-enactment of two foundational moments in Italian history: Caesar's crossing of the Rubicon and the march of Garibaldi's Mille. Thus the most modern event was to have its 'traditional' links stressed. The fascists called on its artists and architects to make the exhibition embody the revolutionary rupture supposedly achieved by fascism – a breakthrough into modernity against overwhelming material and historical odds – while simultaneously playing on deeply rooted and traditional cultural patterns. As such the exhibition served as a fulcrum around which two contradictory forces were worked out. On the one hand, the exhibition incorporated a backward-looking nostalgic and monumentalist mode of reception, commemorating the fascist revolution by connecting it to a mythicized version of community and order and thus giving it a certain historical continuity. The 'Roman' columns represented authority, and the walls included lengthy quotations from Cato, Cicero, Augustus, Machiavelli, Guicciardini and Vico. On the other hand, Mussolini's injunction that the exhibition be 'ultramodern' meant that all of the archaic features of the exhibition were modernized and updated to imply that fascism's heritage encompasses the revolution of modernity too. Thus the exhibition accommodated 'a forward-looking "modernistic" mode of reception that experiences the [exhibition] as an event of rupture on the political level, erasure on the historical level, and disorientation and/or rapture on the level of the individual subject'.[26] Visitors described it as being an unfettered futurism, as having a machine-gun effect, or as thrusting the viewer into a vortex.

Misery leads to past times

It is clear, then, that one of the central tensions in fascism is between a certain kind of revolutionary activism, a positive appreciation of modernity and technological advance, on the one hand, and an institutional conservatism, nostalgic lamentation and reactionary turn to the past, on the other. How are we to make sense of the obvious tension between 'conservative' and 'revolution' or between 'reactionary' and 'modernist'? To do so we have to understand the place of myth in fascism, and the role of myth as a response to modernity especially. This leads to the recognition of the importance of the politics of time in fascism. The remainder of this chapter will outline the theoretical basis of this argument, which will be developed further in the next chapter.

As Alice Yaeger Kaplan notes, the supposed contradiction between modernism and anti-modernism in fascism is in many ways a false one.[27] For a start, the mere fact that a piece of legislation, administrative decision or ideological text praises ancient or medieval 'community values' as an ordering principle of society does not mean that it must immediately be identified as 'anti-modern'. In terms of industrialization, the use of pre-modern language and techniques for the integration of classes was an increasingly common practice in *all* industrialized and industrializing nations as they came to share the vision of 'society as factory'. As Tim Mason puts it, in a comment on the Nazi Labour Front but which applies to fascism generally, almost everything that the Labour Front emphasized as the achievements of the Third Reich had been tried prior to 1933, in Germany and elsewhere. 'In view of the identical development of industrial social policies in the larger American and British industries . . . it is scarcely appropriate to label the new management techniques of German industrialists before 1933 as a specifically German archaism'.[28] Inventing traditions is a key tactic of ruling classes in bourgeois society generally.

More importantly, far from being a reaction *against* modern technology and its uses, reactionary modernist protest against the Enlightenment and its prioritizing of violence are in fact part of its cult of technics. Goebbels noted something like this, in the speech cited above identifying technology as the essence of our times. On the one hand, his speech appears anti-modern: 'The danger unquestionably arises that modern technology will make men soulless'. Yet he immediately points out that 'National Socialism never rejected or struggled against technology'. Rather, one of national socialism's main tasks was 'to consciously affirm it [technology], to *fill it inwardly with soul*, to discipline it and to place it in the service of our people and their cultural level'. Fascism, then, discovers

> *a new romanticism in the results of modern inventions and technology.* While bourgeois reaction was alien to and filled with incomprehension, if not outright hostility to technology, and while modern skeptics believed the deepest roots of the collapse of European culture lay in it, National Socialism understood how to take the soulless framework of technology and fill it with the rhythm and hot impulses of our time.[29]

Fascism not only embraces technology but also fetishizes it, making it central to the politics of destruction. Those who claim that fascism is anti-modern rest their argument on the fact that fascism is not progressive, where 'progressive' implies a commitment to a humane and even socialist future; clearly fascism is not progressive in this sense.[30] But 'modernity' generates opposing forces, forces of reaction as well as progress: we need to take account of the dialectic of modernity as we do the dialectic of Enlightenment. The reactionary forces generated by modernity use the trappings of modernity without subscribing to the Enlightenment idea of progress and the desire for a rational society. Fascism appropriates technology for the nation and war, drawing technology into the service of universal war. Yet this merely furthers the experience of social dislocation as the essence of modernity. The problem of how this social dislocation is to be resolved is not overcome by insisting that we can 'fill technology with soul'. As Brecht put it: '700 intellectuals worshipping an oil-tank', invoking the tank to 'extinguish our selves, make us collective', is hardly sufficient grounds for social order.[31]

We are touching here on the central question of modernity for the political right: how is order maintained in a world of constant change and thus disorder? As Habermas notes, the cult of the new and the exultation of the present, the new value placed in the transitory, the elusive and the ephemeral, the very celebration of dynamism, frequently disclose a longing for an undefiled, immaculate and stable present.[32] The social dislocation of modernity, then, needs to be dealt with politically. Broadly speaking, there are three ways the political right – both fascist and non-fascist – does this. First, by seeking to overcome the effects of capitalism – alienation and class divisions – ideologically. Second, through a strong state and powerful leadership, strong enough to maintain order amidst the constant flux of change. Hence the primacy of politics. These two have been dealt with in previous chapters. Third, by invoking a return to past values, to a social and moral order prior to the current one of constant change, in which social unity existed. Nostalgically invoking the past and images of the past is a central feature of the political right generally and fascism in particular; in doing so, the centrality of the nation and nature to fascist theory and practice is reiterated and consolidated, for the central myths invoked and the traditions invented either are *national* ones or concern some kind of repressed *natural* essence waiting to be reborn in the modern world. For this reason – though not for this reason alone – fascist modernity is simultaneously a world of myth.

In his account of the effect of the First World War on modern memory, Paul Fussell notes that the shocking experiences of new warfare technology pushed soldiers back on to myth as a mechanism for survival.

> A world of reinvigorated myth . . . a throwback way across the nineteenth and eighteenth centuries to Renaissance and medieval modes of thought and feeling. That such a myth-ridden world could take shape in the midst of a war representing a triumph of modern industrialism, materialism, and mechanism is an anomaly worth considering. The result of inexpressible terror long and inexplicably endured is . . . a plethora of very un-modern superstitions, talismans, wonders, miracles, relics, legends, and rumours.[33]

We can expand this point beyond the horrors of the First World War: one of the responses to an unstable world, where the experience of modernity is the experience of instability, social dislocation and the permanent possibility of violent death – misery, in other words – is the desire for the stability thought to have existed in a mythicized harmonious past.

Now, what is partly at issue here is a question of temporality. Roger Griffin has identified fascism as a political ideology whose mythic core is a palingenetic form of populist ultranationalism. Etymologically 'palingenetic' derives from the Greek words *palin* (again, anew) and *genesis* (creation, birth). Though this seems to suggest that 'palingenetic political myth' refers to a backward-looking nostalgia for a restoration of the past (in the sense of *rebirth*), Griffin rightly points to the fact that it refers to the *future* as much as the past. 'The arrow of time thus points not backwards but forwards, even when the archer looks over his shoulder for guidance on where to aim'. Thus the cult of the *romanità*, for example, while appearing to be a reactionary turn to the past, in fact constitutes an orientation to the future. The spirit of eternal Rome was invoked not to regress to a previous civilization, but to encourage Italians to become a new race, a reborn great people.[34] In other words, what appears to be a tension between the past and present is in fact indicative of an orientation towards the future. It is for this reason that so much fascist language and imagery is of the *new* – a new man, new order – though not without some connection to the old – regeneration, resurrection, restoration. At the heart of reactionary modernism is thus a politics of time.

It is this politics of time which produces what Peter Osborne has identified as a paradoxical temporality at the heart of the concepts of 'conservative revolution' and 'reactionary modernism'. Like all fundamental political categories of modernity, conservative revolution is an essentially temporal notion. 'As counter-*revolutionary* ideology, conservative revolution is modernist in the full temporal sense . . . of affirming the temporality of the new. Its image of the future may derive from the mythology of some lost origin or suppressed national essence, but its temporal dynamic is rigorously futural'. Yet conservative revolution is simultaneously a form of revolutionary *reaction*.

> It understands that what it would 'conserve' is already lost (if indeed it ever existed, which is doubtful) and hence must be created anew. It recognizes that under such circumstances the chance presents itself to realize this 'past' *for the first time*. The fact that the past is imaginary is thus no impediment to its political force, but rather its very condition (myth).[35]

Like the old Roman god, Janus, who stood above gateways with one face looking forward and the other backward, fascism also faces both ways at once. That this is so should not surprise us, for the tendency to point to a glorious yet lost past which is nevertheless about to be reborn in an ever more glorious future is also the constitutive feature of nationalism.[36]

Fascism recognizes the emancipatory potential of technology and the fact that the imperative to innovate present in modernity facilitates visions of a radically different future. But bereft of any means for articulating such a vision of its own, it can only hark back to a mythic past. Unable truly to emancipate human beings from the miseries of modernity, fascism can only hanker after a pre-modern time to gloss over this misery: misery leads to past times.[37] It is this which supplies fascism its revolutionary moment. Whereas some political forces on the right wish merely to preserve social order – conservatism, for example, seeks to regulate and manage social discontent by incorporating gradual and piecemeal change into its historical vision – a reactionary modernist politics pits itself against the social order, demanding radical change on the basis of its vision of a mythic past. Whereas conservatism attempts to oversee the dislocating effects of modernity by politically administering the working class inside the body politic, fascism exploits the dynamics of modernity by mobilizing the masses behind its reactionary politics.[38] This mystifies technology: instead of being used for emancipatory purposes, to bring an end to class domination and the system of private property, technology is appropriated for the politics of reaction and the purposes of destruction.

Fascism is the end-point of reactionary counter-revolutionary thought against the Enlightenment, realized in the radically altered political conditions of the twentieth century. Being a movement of modernity, for modernity, and yet against the emancipatory potential of modernity, fascist reactionary modernism mobilizes the masses against themselves. It captures human desire for a different – and radically better – world but, abandoning the political and philosophical project of Enlightenment and emancipation, it refuses to let rationalization become truly rational. Fascism has to resist the realization of the emancipatory potential implicit in modernity, as this would mean the end of fascism. Because rationalization has yet to become truly rational, the traces of the old world cannot but appear to be an improvement on our current state. Fascism, refusing to participate in the construction of a rational society, but none the less capturing the desire for such a rational society, can do nothing other than try to recapture a mythic past, conceived as a glorious and homogeneous national and natural order. As Adorno writes, in the face of present misery, older forms of immediacy, no matter how outdated and questionable they may be, acquire a certain rightfulness.

> As long as the face of the earth keeps being ravished by utilitarian pseudo-progress, it will turn out to be impossible to disabuse human intelligence of the notion that, despite all the evidence to the contrary, the pre-modern world was better and more humane, its backwardness notwithstanding.[39]

The Iron Logic of Nature

There are grounds for fascism to think of the nation as a *natural* entity rather than an imagined community: *nasci* – to be born – is the root of both 'nature' and 'nation', providing an etymological justification for thinking of the nation as a natural form for living communities to take; we still talk of the process of becoming a member of the nation as one of 'naturalization'. 'Nature' has of course been present in the argument throughout this book: the will, struggle, war, race are all integrally linked to ideas about the natural. For fascism, it is a straightforward fact that nature operates according to what Hitler describes as 'stern and rigid laws'.[1] It is according to these laws that we should live, for they apply equally to the social world. This approach to society is based on a crude social Darwinism, which involves a direct and unmediated application of biological and pseudo-biological categories to the social realm.[2] When the fascist talks of the laws of nature there are in fact three related issues at stake. First, there is the fact that for fascism the social body is a natural body. Those who have taken on board Enlightenment rationalism have thought of the social order as somehow human-made, susceptible to manipulation on the basis of reason, and have therefore failed to comprehend the natural laws which society must follow. Second, those in the Enlightenment tradition derogate nature itself, thinking of nature as there for man's benefit and subject to man's manipulation; they have thus destroyed nature, polluting it by trying to dominate it. Third, this pollution of nature is because the same people have polluted the concept of nature. This has allowed nature itself to be destroyed and society to be planned according to decisions which are 'against nature'.

Landscapes and bodies

Focusing on the natural allows fascism to highlight the issue of land
and its importance to the people and nation.[3] The Nazi 'blood and
soil' doctrine, for example, is suggestive of an intimate connection
between the blood of the people (nation) and the soil of the land
(nature), expressing the unity of a racial people and its land.
Because of this, some forms of fascism focus on the peasantry and
agriculture as the most powerful expression of blood and soil. For
Nazism, agricultural policies were of fundamental importance, and
not merely to attract the peasantry into support for the movement
and regime. It is only through respect for the land that a social order
can be maintained. The Nazi ideologue, Walther Darré, for
example, uses arguments about natural forces to provide the basis
for a Nazi approach to agriculture and land policy in which the
peasant is to be revered for being closer to the earth, working with
nature to produce basic commodities for the people. It is the
peasant that should be saluted as the life of the nation, being the key
link between nature and production.[4]

My concern here is not the degree to which fascism in power
implemented such policies, but to identify the green thread running
through fascist thought and to trace this thread back to the idea of
nature. The green thread appears straightforwardly environmental-
ist – a demand that we take seriously the exploitation and
destruction of the land by industrial development and modernization – but ideologically fascism does not merely 'respect' nature: it
sanctifies and spiritualizes it. For fascism the philosophical distinction between man and nature is an artificial product of rationalist
philosophy and science. For the Nazis especially, the concept of
'humanity' is biological nonsense, for man, 'species-man', is part of
nature. This essentially religious conception uses the idea of nature
to overcome problematic philosophical and theological dualisms, as
well as the confrontation between science and religion, not,
however, by suggesting that man may dominate nature, but by
positing 'nature' as the subject of unity and the giver of the laws of
life: witness Martin Boorman's suggestion that in place of God and
any ideas of divine humanity, Nazism puts life itself. This in effect
downgrades man: 'Man is nothing special, nothing more than a
piece of earth', Himmler tells us.[5]

Sanctifying nature as a universal force encourages the belief that nature is the foundation of national unity. Saving nature from its polluters, protecting the land from destruction, is a means by which the nation is to be protected from its polluters and destroyers. In this sense fascism is a synthesis of nationalism and naturalism, a 'life-bound nationalism'. The sanctification of nature is simultaneously the sanctification of the nation as the natural collective unit.[6] The integral connection between the idea of a national spirit and the spiritual concept of nature focuses attention on *this* nature, that is, the land of *this* nation, and the role it plays in shaping national character and identity. A geographically specific nature forms the mediating link between the sanctification of nature and the nationalist impulse in fascist thought.

In national socialism this meant appropriating themes and arguments from the conservationist and *völkisch* movements. The following passage from a woodlands preservation outfit gives a flavour of the conceptual links between nature and nation:

> In every German breast the German forest quivers with its caverns and ravines, crags and boulders, waters and winds, legends and fairy tales, with its songs and its melodies, and awakens a powerful yearning and a longing for home; in all German souls the German forest lives . . . it is the source of German inwardness, of the German soul, of German freedom. Therefore protect and care for the German forest.[7]

The juxtaposition and repetition of 'German' alongside 'forest' and in connection with the idea of spirit fuses together nationalism and naturalism in a form of mythical enchantment.[8] The idea that the natural environment is a source of national character oscillates between the universal claim that one should think in terms of man-in-nature as opposed to man and nature as autonomous realms, and the more particular claim that man in this particular nature necessarily ('naturally') develops in a certain way, with a certain character and subject to a certain collective longing and belonging. Thus the primary purpose of the protection of nature is in fact the protection of the nation. As Darré puts it, 'To remove the German soul from the natural landscape is to kill it'.[9] Part of the thinking behind the construction of the motorway network throughout Germany, for example, was that although the motorway system was expected to unify the nation it should nevertheless follow the natural lines of the countryside in order that this modern transportation system gave the impression of 'closeness to nature'. Given the predominant idea that nature was a realm distinct from humankind, the motorway had to have the appearance of being shaped according to the natural contours of German land. The unification of the nation had to be achieved in harmony with nature.[10]

Anna Bramwell claims that the Nazis were alone among fascist parties in expressing ecological concerns to the extent that they did. It is clear that agriculture and the peasantry played a far less significant role in other forms of fascism. While fascism generally pays at least lip-service to the peasantry and ecological concerns, only the Nazis made the peasantry a central plank of their policies and ecological concerns a major ideological issue. The Nazis also saw other fascisms as too 'inorganic', too concerned with culture rather than nature. One of the main reasons for this is said to be the fact that only the Nazis possessed what has been described as a 'religion of nature'. Whereas Nazism clearly sanctifies nature, other fascisms appear to deny the existence of an absolute nature, focusing instead on culture and a conception of spirit not dependent on a related concept of nature. The claim, in other words, is that there is a radical disjuncture between Nazism and fascism which rests on their conceptions of nature.[11] But Bramwell misconstrues the place of nature in fascism, relying far too heavily on a distinction between nature and culture. For the Nazis the forest is not merely nature, but culture too. Because the natural myth is a national myth, the mythical enchantment of the forest is as much a cultural process as it is a paean to nature. Moreover, too great a focus on the actual content of the fascist policies obscures the common ideological presuppositions behind them. To be sure, the sanctification of nature takes different forms in fascism, and feeds into fascist concepts of the social and determines fascist practice in different ways, but no fascist would dispute Hitler's claim that 'when man attempts to rebel against *the iron logic of Nature*, he comes into struggle with the principles to which he himself owes his existence as a man'.[12]

The point is not how concepts of nature affect policy, but to recognize the importance of nature to fascist myth, for to invoke the iron logic of nature is to invoke a joint myth: of nature's mobility – constant change, struggle and perpetual war – and nature's immobility – natural (universal) law. The purpose of myth is to 'legitimize factuality'; it is for this reason that myth is central to bourgeois ideology. Fascist myth legitimizes factuality in a recourse to nature, giving historical intention a natural justification, making contingency appear eternal. Having emptied reality of history, fascist myth fills it with nature.[13] The fundamental historicity of nation, state, private property and patriarchy is shattered, conceived of instead as prior to society, primal givens which thus become unquestionable; understanding the historical causes of war is abandoned in favour of the belief that war is natural.

The centrality of nature to fascism is manifest in the clash between being and thinking, between will and reason, and between instinctive allegiance and considered solidarity. Nowhere is this more explicit than in questions of sexuality and gender, for as George Mosse notes, 'the basic view of woman was more alike than different among the various brands of European fascism'.[14] By articulating nature as a standard by which the social order can be judged, the success of the nation becomes dependent on the acceptance of natural laws relating to sexuality and gender. The basic view identified by Mosse as common to fascism combines the claim that there are 'natural' gender roles with an illiberal struggle against 'deviant' sexual practices and their justification by liberal intellectuals. For fascism, the natural order clearly distinguishes between men and women on the basis of their propensities and sensitivities. This provides fascism with the grounds for distinguishing the normal from the abnormal, where the abnormal is read as a threat to the natural – and thus the national – order.

Looking back to a golden age in which each sex exhibited its natural characteristics, fascism places the abandonment of these characteristics at the heart of modern decadence and national decline; it is the abandonment of these roles that has also given rise to a conflict between men and women. For Hitler, 'a conflict between the sexes . . . is impossible as long as each fulfils the task set to it by nature'.[15] As with all reactionary politics, fascism considers the essential role of women to be the production of children, and their place at home within the family unit. For fascism, biology really is destiny. Where men are destined for war, women are destined for motherhood: 'War is to man what maternity is to a woman'.[16] It is undoubtedly the case that this view of woman is meant as a means of sustaining traditional structures of male domination, but this fascist image of the natural role for women is also rooted in the question of national power. Behind the biological destiny of women lies the biological destiny of the nation, for behind the concern for women's place in society is the assumption that the family is the root of nation and state. By reviving more traditional and 'natural' ways, the nation can regain that lost unity and harmony between the sexes. Women are thus reproducers of the nation. The size, vigour and general well-being of the nation is thus dependent on the size, vigour and general well-being of the family, in which women play a pivotal role. Claims that 'a Nation without mothers and without cradles . . . is condemned to moral, political and economic decline and is certainly headed for slavery' and that 'with each child she [woman] brings into the world for the nation, she is fighting her struggle for the nation' are as much a paean to the nation and the importance of motherhood to the nation as they are to motherhood *per se*.[17] Hence the emphasis on Mother's Day as a celebration of the place of mothers in perpetuating and defending the nation rather than a chance for a sentimental 'thank you' to be made to mums everywhere.

For this reason fascism possesses another perception of woman: as a militant citizen actively involved (in a decidedly non-maternal fashion) in the maintenance of the regime. This perception is intimately connected with the perception of the nation at war and total mobilization. Maria Fraddosio writes that:

> The model of the *woman-soldier*, quite apart from what it managed to achieve in the event, was an ideal prototype, the expression of a mentality and a line of conduct which, without in the least sacrificing femininity, was closest to those standards of 'virility', such as resilience and courage, which were recognized as the typical values of the fascist ethos and considered to be specifically 'male' by tradition.[18]

Fraddosio's claim, intended as an account of a specific period in the history of Italian fascism, holds true for fascism generally. Alongside the image of woman as mother and wife exists an image of women as *fighters* for the nation. The fascist 'liberation' grants them a place at the heart of the struggle for the nation. Its image of woman as reproducer is not tarnished by thinking of them in marching boots instead of sensible shoes, or throwing the javelin instead of doing the washing.[19]

To describe this as a kind of 'secondary racism', as some have done, is misleading.[20] For fascism, woman is not a threat *as woman*, in the way that Jews or blacks are a threat as Jews or blacks. It is a certain *type* of woman that constitutes the threat. Klaus Theweleit's account of the male fantasies which shape the formation of fascism reveal a fear of the sexually active, lipstick- and rouge-wearing woman, on the one hand, exemplifying the decadence of the modern bourgeois world, and, on the other, the feminist who questions the nature of sexual division and the patriarchal social order. These two figures constitute a threat by insisting that the 'natural' order is in fact an artificial structure of (male) power. By challenging this structure of male power they challenge, in different ways, one of the 'natural' forms of domination. And by challenging the fascist view of sexuality they appear to be condoning free love, sexual diversity and experimentation. Feminism is thus unnatural. For these reasons the feminist woman is a proletarian whore (sexually active) and a vehicle for communism (a threat to traditional structures of domination). For fascism, 'proletarian whore' and 'female communist' are interchangeable terms. The communist threat is thus not only *political* – an attempt to transform the natural structures of domination and authority – but also *sexual* – the liberation of the senses and human desire.[21] To the extent that feminism participates in the movement for the liberation of human desires, as well as the challenge to political authority, it too is communist.

Fascism's myth of nature and demand for a return to traditional gender roles is a response to the misery and anxiety generated by modernity – urban disengagement, sexual frustration and social alienation. Unable to project a way out of this, fascism seeks a revival of more 'natural' forms of social process seemingly lost from history: urban disengagement to be replaced by community and solidarity of the countryside; sexual frustration and conflict to be resolved by return to 'normal' male–female relations; social alienation to be overcome in a return to past glories. Once again fascism's response to the miseries of the present is a reactionary movement against the emancipatory potential implicit in modernity and for a return to a mythic past.

The gaze of the coffin maker

The fascist fear of feminism and deviant sexuality rests, in turn, on conceptions of the human and social body, a 'politics of the body', through an obsession with virility and the health of each member of the society and, relatedly, a vision of society as a collective body. Mediating between these two issues is the body of the leader, at once both an individual human being and, as representative and leader of the nation, representative of the virility and health of the nation.

Fascism's overt anti-intellectualism, glorification of the will and reification of war is compounded by the glorification of the body and its force which, since Nietzsche, has come to signify the domain of the irrational and the vehicle of the expression of will. In a speech at a gymnastics festival in July 1933, Hitler decried the 'so-called Age of Reason':

> The over-valuation of knowledge led not merely to a disregard of the bodily form and bodily strength, but in the end to a lack of respect for bodily work. It is not chance that this age, propagated and protected by sick persons, necessarily led to a general sickness – not only to sickness of the body but also to sickness of the mind. For he who despises bodily strength and health has already become the victim of a malformation of the intellect.[22]

The sovereignty of the body is thus invested with the sacred authority of instinct. This fetishization of the body and the aesthetics of physical perfection and stylish virility are specific to fascism and the fascist political project. It is partly a result of treating the human body as a 'political space', as the Nazi sports theorist, Alfred Baeumler, puts it. A major feature of Pierre Drieu La Rochelle's work, for example, is what he called the 'revolution of the body', the 'great revolution of the twentieth century' which will usher in the new man by restoring the values of the body. 'What I like about fascism', he says, 'is a certain virile disposition. It has come about . . . as the result of a certain physical need in man. This need is satisfied when man has the impression of having pushed his body as far as his ideas'.[23] And the Parti Populaire Française declared its social and economic programme to be directed in its entirety towards 'the athletic transformation of man'.[24]

As a political space the body can be inscribed with a certain set of power relations taken from predetermined conceptions of bodily health and strength. By then applying these to the collective body of the nation, fascism takes organicism to its logical conclusion. The means of rejuvenating and defending the nation lie in virilizing it, putting the life back into it and making it strong and healthy once more. Filippo Marinetti compares the Italian people with an 'excellent wrestler', Robert Brasillach compares the unity of the nation with the unity of a sports team, Baeumler thinks of the collective body of the *Volk* as a political team, and Oswald Mosley describes the corporate fascist state as 'a state organised like a human body'. As John Hoberman notes, it is because organicists require assurance that the collective body is not degenerating that images gleaned from physical fitness and training are appropriated as a means of thinking through the politics of the collective body.[25] It is in this context that the health and virility of the leadership is of crucial importance. Despite the fact that most fascist leaders fail to conform to their own stereotypical conceptions of the virile body, they nevertheless think of themselves as the best example of new fascist man. Mussolini's dream of having his ministers hurdle through flaming hoops is surpassed only by his own tendency to go running stripped to the waist.[26] And this is undoubtedly how fascists see their own leaders. Witness Marinetti's description of Mussolini as exemplifying the highest form of 'physiological patriotism':

> because physically he is built *all'italiana*, designed by inspired and brutal hands, forged, carved to the model of the mighty rocks of our peninsula . . . Bent over his desk on large elbows, his arms as alert as levers, he threatens to leap across his papers at any pest or enemy. A swing of the agile torso from left to right, to brush off trivial things. Rising to speak, he bends forward his masterful head, like a squared-off projectile, a package full of good gunpowder, the cubic will of the State.

Or consider Drieu's description of the leader of the Parti Populaire Française, Jacques Doriot, as 'big and strong. Everything about him breathes health and plenitude: his abundant hair, his powerful shoulders'.[27]

The obsession with the health of the collective body is part of the fascist revival of pre-modern conceptions of society and politics. As Ernst Kantorowicz shows in his account of *The King's Two Bodies*, the image of the king's body as a double body – the mortal, corporeal body of the king contrasted with the immortal body which can never legally die – was central to medieval political theology because it provided a mechanism for thinking through the relationship between the individual and the collective, which was at once spiritual and corporeal.[28] The king possessed the power to incarnate in his body the community of the kingdom and invest it with a sacred power. This way of thinking about the collective died away with the breakdown of feudalism and the triumph of liberal democracy.[29] As the body politic expanded in size, incorporating within it the working class, political thought largely gave up the attempt to understand it through medieval concepts. The fascist revival of this way of thinking about the nation – as a collective body shot through with sacred meaning, bound into the body of the leader and given historical permanence by being invested with spirit – is thus a revival of a medieval thought applied to modern mass politics.

The focus on the health and virility of the collective body necessarily leads to an equally powerful obsession with the sickness of the nation. The aestheticization of the body provides the basis for the disparagement of non-fascist writers and enemy movements, variously described as weak, flabby, shoddy, sickly, effeminate and pathetic. For Mosley, Britain had turned into an old woman, whilst José Antonio Primo de Rivera calls the opponents of his father's dictatorship 'cripples'.[30] French socialists, says Pierre Drieu La Rochelle, concern themselves 'with the sexual and moral liberty of man, but not with his physical liberty, which is his health'. And he goes on: 'One only has to look at them to realize . . . Attend a socialist convention and look at all the beards, all the bellies, the tobacco smoke, the anxious anticipation of the before-dinner drink'.[31] Replicating bourgeois flabbiness and sickliness, the opponents of fascism, and Marxist opponents in particular, reveal a fundamental lack of will and virility. Here biological categories are simultaneously political ones: 'impotent', for example, applies to both sexuality and politics. And for the Nazis, 'Jewish' was a sexual word (they dissolve our bodies), a political word (they dissolve our state through Bolshevism), and an economic word (they liquidate our money; they swim in it; we have nothing).[32] Beyond the deprecation of oppositional movements, such comments reveal the essence of the fascist sanctification of the laws of nature.

The concept of 'nature' is, of course, deeply problematical, subject as it is to a wide scope of meanings that make it, in essence, an empty vessel to be filled with whatever meaning is politically expedient. It is for this reason that much of the recent social and political theory which deals with the question of nature has veered towards constructionist accounts of the natural. Those which do not, which instead think of nature as a subject in itself, run the constant risk of subscribing to reactionary political views – deep ecology is a case in point.[33] This is not simply because of the kind of authoritarian political structures which would be necessary to carry out the environmental changes demanded. It is also because 'nature' acts as a register of changing conceptions as to who qualifies for full membership of the *human* community, as Kate Soper has noted.[34] But decisions concerning such qualifications are of necessity *political* ones. Given its social Darwinism, fascism assumes that in a truly natural society the universal war will destroy everything sickly, weak or diseased. Modern society, it claims, has perverted this natural course of events, encouraging the care and preservation not of the healthy and virile but of the sickly and weak, even allowing them into positions of power. Thus what should be a natural development – the survival of the fittest through struggle and war – must be politically engineered. State power must be used to return to natural law.

In this context the invidious tone of Walther Darré's account of the protection and cultivation of natural forms becomes clear. Citing Frederick the Great's claim that too much time is spent cultivating bananas and pineapples in rough northern climates when not enough is being done to cultivate humans, Darré insists that it is impossible to create an aristocracy without *breeding* it into existence. That the idea of breeding should be applied as much to humans as to plants has been lost with the rise of Enlightenment humanitarianism and its claims about man and nature; the subsequent decline in national character and power has been all too evident.

> Thus we are facing the realization that questions of breeding are not trivial for political thought, but that they have to be at the centre of all considerations . . . We must even assert that a people can only reach spiritual and moral equilibrium if a well-conceived breeding plan stands at the very *centre* of its culture.

Because society is a natural body, we should adopt methods used for maintaining and cultivating natural forms. Society is like a garden; gardens produce weeds, threatening the health of the garden as a whole. As well as breeding the right species, then, gardeners must also be willing to engage in weeding, digging out alien species which have developed from within and which threaten to consume the whole.

> He who leaves the plants in a garden to themselves will soon find to his surprise that the garden is overgrown by weeds and that even the basic

character of the plants has changed. If therefore the garden is to
remain the breeding ground for plants . . . then the forming will of a
gardener is necessary, a gardener who . . . ruthlessly eliminates the
weeds.[35]

The double meaning of the word 'weed' – its reference, on the one
hand, to a wild plant growing where it is not wanted, and, on the
other hand, to a weak or sickly person – is remarkably appropriate
in this context, for fascism rests on the belief that a process of
weeding out from the social body those who are unwanted – in other
words, the elimination of those objects not fit to live in the
community – is an entirely legitimate political exercise. Such
elimination takes the form of either gardening – weeding out the
unwanted – or social prophylaxis – expelling waste matter as a
means of cleansing the body.

By failing to achieve the required standard of respectability,
those who engage in *unnatural* sexual acts fail to qualify for
membership of the *human* community.[36] The battle fascism wages
against the diversity of human desire involves encoding this desire
with a particular set of attributes – sickness, effeminacy, crimi-
nality, Jewishness (all of which exist together under the umbrella of
'communism') – and targets state power against it.[37] Those who
engage in unnatural acts are conceived of as either outside of nature
and thus may be exterminated, or as germs within the social body in
which case they should be purged. (The idea of 'purging' has an
appropriate mix of political and biological connotations here.) In
either case, sexual contact with them runs the risk of granting them
an entry point into the social body: sexual contact with other races
contaminates the pure race with the blood of the impure. Syphilis,
identified by J.P. Stern as Hitler's most obsessive fear, plays a
crucial role in fascist ideology because it expresses the danger of
physical degeneration – of both individual and collective – brought
about through sexual contact with those who fall outside the circle
of respectability or are somehow beyond nature, that is, non-
human. Syphilis, as Theweleit puts it, is not something one *has*, but
is either a condition deliberately *given* or a function of enemy
intelligence.[38] The concept of syphilis, as appropriated for fascist
ideology, rests on prior assumptions about who is part of the social
body and facilitates the slippage between questions of sexuality and
the political and economic threat to the nation.

The ostensible purpose of fascism is, on the one hand, to create a new man – healthy, virile, capable, wilful, full of life: a superman. The underside of this is that the cultivation and breeding of this new race of aristocratic supermen necessarily conceives of some humans as outside nature. For all the fascist talk of creating new men, the result is the treatment of some humans as less than animals, or even plants, which are at least part of nature. And the result of conceiving some human beings as less than animals is their treatment as *objects* – to be measured, tested, experimented on. The net effect of treating some people as sub-human objects of administration rather than as human subjects in their own right, is the policy of deliberate death: in this the human body remains a corpse, no matter how fit and healthy it is trained to be.[39]

This is the real basis and function of the role of nature and the natural in fascism. For the 'return' to nature is a return to pre-civilized forms of sociality; a return, that is, to barbarism. Because civilization is thought to have failed, and appears to offer no means to escape this failure, only barbarism is left, couched in the language of the 'new man' and dressed in the garb of nature. Unable truly to liberate human desire and emancipate humanity from forces of exploitation and practices of domination currently in existence, the fascist invokes nature as a means of crushing human desire. The central aim of fascist discourse on the body is thus the death of sexuality.[40] It is the taming of the masses in the sexual sphere. The love of nature in fascist propaganda is a veiled reaction to failed civilization, a reactionary turn against the failure truly to liberate the human senses.

Those who extol the body above all else invariably have the closest affinity with killing; the lovers of nature are often also the most vicious killers.[41] 'They see the body as a moving mechanism', Adorno and Horkheimer write, 'with joints as its components and flesh to cushion the skeleton. They use the body and its parts as though they were already separated from it'. It is this separation, this distance, this alienation, which allows fascism to treat the human subject as object. Adorno and Horkheimer continue: 'Jewish tradition contains a disinclination to measure men with a foot-rule because the corpse is measured this way for the coffin. This is what the manipulators of the body enjoy. They measure others . . . with the gaze of a coffin maker'.[42] The most untrammelled nature is war itself. In transposing the 'laws of nature' on to the social realm and reading the latter as a realm of perpetual war, the struggle for survival, fascism points in two directions: first, the measurement, comparison, statistical analysis and administration of the distinction between the normal and the pathological, the natural and the unnatural; and second, the identification of the unnatural as alien and thus inimical, often conceived of as internal to the social body. Both these directions have the same end-point: the brutalization of the human body and desire, and, ultimately, slaughter – the first because the bureaucratic high point of the identification of the unnatural and pathological must be the elimination of the enemy; the second because the existential high point of the identification of war as a perpetual phenomenon of the social body is death of the enemy. Fascism is an ideology obsessed with death; 'I kill, therefore I am. I die, therefore I was' its central philosophical principle.[43] The highest achievement of fascism, then, is a pile of corpses, its history a catalogue of human destruction.

Conclusion

In 1988 Albion Press published John Tyndall's *The Eleventh Hour: A Call for British Rebirth*. Written while in prison for breaking the Public Order Act by publishing words liable to promote racial hatred, the book's 'nationalist' analysis of the contemporary political situation articulates themes which I have identified as central to fascism: the 'cancer' of liberalism, the weakness of conservative elites, the parliamentary and party roots of the British sickness, the perversion of communism and internationalism, and the policy of the British National Party to be 'beyond capitalism and socialism'.[1] Set alongside increased attacks by fascist thugs on immigrants and racial minorities, the desecration of Jewish graves and cemeteries, and an increased vote for fascist parties (or what look like fascist parties even though they may eschew the designation 'fascist') in a variety of countries, such publications lend weight to the claim that fascism is returning. Examination of the fascist or neo-fascist nature of organizations of the far right has been performed well enough by others.[2] My concern here is with the question of the *return* of fascism which, it seems to me, rests on the mistaken belief that the collapse of fascist *regimes* represented the death of fascism; it mistakes the regime for the ideology and movement. It is impossible to say that fascism ever died as an ideology. Fascist regimes were defeated, but fascism lived on, and continues to live on, in ideas and arguments. Since fascism never died, it does not need to be 'reborn'.[3]

One of the claims in this book has been that the problem of fascism is the problem of our *lived* relations, for fascism is a response to key features of modern society. The fact that fascism lives on is a result of the continued existence of the same alienated lived relations, the same objective conditions that brought about fascism in the first place.[4] These include, generally, the continued domination of capitalism as the world historical form and the crises inherent in that system, the hegemony of liberalism and liberal democratic ideas, the socialist and communist movements which capitalism gives rise to, the range of racial, anti-Semitic and sexual prejudices that arise in a multi-cultural society simultaneously torn apart by social contradiction, a society in which rationalization has not yet become truly rational.

And yet these historical conditions are in many ways so very *different* from the inter-war period. Several features stand out. Most important is the collapse of the Soviet Union which fascists (as well as conservatives, liberals and, unfortunately, some sections of the left) saw as the vanguard of communism. In the absence of any real communist or Soviet threat there appears to be no need for any national bourgeoisie and ruling elite to turn to fascism as a last-ditch attempt to avoid communism. Moreover, the period since 1945 has been a period of extended peace (at least relative to the 1920s), of increased prosperity, and of the successful political management of crises by the ruling elites of capitalist society. These factors are, of course, mutually interdependent. With the absence of any real communist threat the management of crises is both easier and less fraught with danger.

The above factors are fairly widely accepted by commentators on fascism.[5] The remarks which follow are designed to proffer a further explanation for the failure of fascism to win power over the last two or three decades and to suggest reasons why we should not take it for granted that this failure will continue. The comments are therefore of a speculative nature.

One possible factor in the failure of fascist ideas to take hold in the post-war period may well lie in the increased radicalism of parties and organizations of the non-fascist right. If it is the case that fascism is a form of reactionary modernism and has integral links with demands for a conservative revolution, then a crucial factor in the success or failure of fascism will be the relative radicalism of conservatism and, concomitantly, conservative elites. The fact that some forms of conservatism have become increasingly radical in the last two or more decades may well mean that individuals, organizations, ruling classes and governing elites which in other circumstances may have looked to fascism as a solution to the crises of contemporary capitalism have in fact been swayed from this by the radicalization of some forms of contemporary conservatism. This argument depends on how one understands the project of the New Right. Many have noted the radicalism of the New Right, and have assumed that this radicalism stems from the attempt at *modernizing* Western liberal democracies. But in fact the New Right has been radical not because it sought the 'modernization' of liberal democratic states and societies, but because its project has been essentially *reactionary*: it pitted itself against the existing order – the post-war 'consensus' regarding welfarism and the quasi-corporate management of capitalism – in the light of an image of past national glory (a mythic and contradictory image, but no less powerful for that). The central elements of New Right politics – an aggressive leadership, uncompromising stance on law and order, illiberal attitude on moral questions generally and certain political questions such as race and immigration, an attack on the labour movement and a defence of private property, and a forthright nationalism – all combine in a politics of *reaction*: a reassertion of the principle of private property and capital accumulation as the *raison d'être* of modern society, alongside an authoritarian moralism requiring excessive state power as a means of policing civil society.[6] If there is such a thing as the New Right distinct from 'traditional' conservatism, then it lies in its being a reactionary modernism of our times.[7]

The radicalism of the New Right project had a wide appeal to forces and movements of the right more generally. In the case of Britain, for example, the success of the Conservative Party in Britain from 1979 coincided with the relative decline of the National Front, of which John Tyndall was a formative figure. Formed in 1967, the National Front had 12 years of success – if measured in terms of votes won in elections and the extent of media attention received – before entering into a decline and then a series of splits from 1979.[8] This decline is undoubtedly partly an effect of the strong opposition to the National Front by organizations established by the British left. But the decline also coincided with the achievement of power by the Conservative Party which subsumed the politics of reaction under the umbrella of the Thatcher government's policies. If this claim has any substance then one of the major obstacles to the rise of fascism is precisely the extent to which other forces on the political right engage in a reactionary activism in response to crisis. This certainly has some historical foundation: fascism was successful in those countries where conservative forces turned to fascism as a final solution to the capitalist crises and the bourgeois decadence said to be sapping national strength. This is all heavily dependent on the extent to which forces of the right can tame and dominate the working class.

In considering the contemporary position of fascism one also needs to be aware that the very fact that fascism has in fact been in power in the past transforms the nature of the current debate on fascism entirely, in a number of ways. While the politics of the revolt against positivism and Enlightenment philosophy still play a fundamental role in fascist arguments, the nature of these arguments, and in turn the nature of the debates about fascism, have been reshaped in the light of the experiences of the Italian and German regimes and the Holocaust in particular. The Holocaust has in many ways replaced the Enlightenment as the central issue on which debates about fascism – by both fascists and non-fascists – engage.

The fact that fascists themselves now question the historical reality of the Holocaust – *Did Six Million Really Die?*, *The Hoax of the Century* and *The Auschwitz Myth* are titles of works challenging the social democratic consensus around the Holocaust – should not surprise us, living as we are in the society of the spectacle.[9] The logic of the challenge to the consensus is that the holocaust is largely an invention of the allied forces, liberal and socialist writers and Jewish conspiratorial forces, all engaged in a long-term plan to prevent fascism arising again. The intention behind the challenge is clear: it is to suggest that there is nothing inherent in fascism that leads to mass slaughter, nothing necessarily violent about fascist theory and practice and that to think otherwise – to argue that fascism views human bodies with the gaze of the coffin maker – is merely an attempt to denigrate fascism. But despite the attempt by fascists to present such arguments as intellectually and politically pertinent and thus as academically acceptable – by publishing journals with respectable titles such as the *Journal of Historical Review*, for example – the net effect has really been a series of media *coups* swiftly followed by revelation of the shoddy intellectual work that has produced these arguments.

A related and in some ways far more dangerous trend is the

attempt to 'revise' our understanding of the Holocaust by placing it in the wider context of European history. Ernst Nolte's suggestion that the Holocaust be understood in the context of the widespread practice of genocide, the Soviet extermination of the kulaks and the fact that international Jewish organizations had declared their forthright opposition to Nazism, has the effect of relativizing the Holocaust by making it appear a rather unexceptional event in the context of European history. A similar effect is achieved by Andreas Hillgruber's claim that to come to terms with their past Germans have to recognize that the war meant not only the 'end of European Jewry' but also the 'shattering of the German Reich', thereby placing the Holocaust in the context of the collapse of German power generally. (The two phrases constitute the subtitle of Hillgruber's book, but note how the first event is merely an *ending* whereas the second is a *shattering*, making the latter rather than the former appear the result of forces of destruction). On this reading the 'end' of the Jews is relativized by being presented alongside the 'shattering' of the German Reich.[10]

The Italian revisionist debate, while conducted at an intellectual arm's length from the German, connects up with it politically in an intimate and dangerous way. Largely a product of the intellectual labours of Renzo de Felice, the most influential scholar of Italian fascism, and the struggle of the Movimento Sociale Italiano (Italian Social Movement, MSI) and more recently the Alleanza Nazionale (National Alliance, AN) to win support at the polls, the general thrust of Italian revisionism has been to rehabilitate fascist intellectuals such as Gentile and offer a reading of Mussolini as a major contributor to national greatness whose own status has been undermined by the supposedly crude distortion achieved by the association of Italian fascism with Nazism. Here the denial by some that the term 'fascism' has any meaning outside of the Italian context comes into its own. Freed from any connection with the Nazis – the real bad guys because of their racism and anti-Semitism – our understanding of fascism in Italy is to be 'revised'. De Felice knows full well the political implications of his work: in December 1987 he argued that the time had come to abolish those parts of the Italian constitution which prevented the creation of a fascist party, for two main reasons. First, the constitution did not in fact prevent a fascist party such as the MSI from existing, so it was illogical to pretend that it did. Second, fascism was not responsible for the

Holocaust anyway, and thus should not be held in such low esteem.[11] Hence Gianfranco Fini's insistence, in his days as leader of the MSI, that fascism has nothing to do with anti-Semitism: 'It is shameful to suggest that fascism is or was anti-Semitic – the boys with the shaved heads who commit anti-Jewish acts and say they are fascists have no idea what they are talking about'.[12] This is the crucial intellectual and political background to the current rise of the AN, and the cause for concern. Formed from the MSI and supposedly free of the MSI's fascist roots (but with the blessing of Alessandra Mussolini), the AN retains a fascist core and leader.[13]

It is perhaps worth reminding ourselves of the power of one of George Orwell's messages in *Nineteen Eighty-Four*: who controls the past controls the future; who controls the present controls the past. For whatever the revisionists may claim about the importance of the search for truth and the open nature of academic questions, the effect of revisionism is to write out of history the destructive tendencies of fascism. Set alongside the increasing rehabilitation of thinkers who were once beyond the pale for having played a major role in legitimizing fascism or who, as conservative revolutionaries, were in effect the intellectual vanguard of fascism,[14] the culture of revisionism through which we are living can only be a cause of alarm, for it produces a political and historical forgetting which serves to justify that which is being forgotten. Given the wider context of a political consensus shifting ever further to the right, and the delight some left intellectuals have had in trashing the Enlightenment project in favour of a postmodern politics which renders them unable to cast judgement on revisionism, let alone fascism, this is a dangerous portent of things to come.

Notes

Preface

1 Hugh Trevor-Roper, 'The Phenomenon of Fascism', in Stuart Woolf (ed.), *Fascism in Europe* (London: Methuen, 1981), p. 19.

2 George Lukács, *The Destruction of Reason* (1952), trans. Peter Palmer (London: Merlin Press, 1980), p. 4.

3 Klaus Theweleit, *Male Fantasies, Vol. 2: Male Bodies: Psychoanalyzing the White Terror*, trans. Chris Turner and Erica Carter (Cambridge: Polity Press, 1989), p. 358.

4 Stanley Payne begins *A History of Fascism, 1914–1945* (London: UCL Press, 1995) by pointing out that the bibliography pertaining to the history of fascism is enormous, and that to read everything would take several decades in itself; one does not get the feeling that he is exaggerating. Ian Kershaw, in *The Nazi Dictatorship: Problems and Perspectives of Interpretation* (London: Edward Arnold, 1985), p. 3, honestly admits that 'the extent of the literature on Nazism is so vast that even experts have difficulty coping'.

5 Gilbert Allardyce, 'What Fascism Is Not: Thoughts on the Deflation of a Concept', *American Historical Review*, vol. 84, no. 2, 1979, p. 388.

6 A similar approach is made by Paul Gilroy, 'Revolutionary Conservatism and the Tyrannies of Unanism', *New Formations*, 28, 1996, p. 75. My comment here is meant to suggest that I am treating fascism as any 'ism' should be treated: as a heuristic construction, the value of which derives from generating more insights than confusion (see Roger Eatwell, 'Towards a New Model of Generic Fascism', *Journal of Theoretical Politics*, vol. 4, no. 2, 1992, p. 167). It should also suggest that my treatment of fascism will, hopefully, provide some insights regarding modernity and capitalism.

7 Susan Sontag, 'Fascinating Fascism', in Susan Sontag, *Under the Eye of Saturn* (New York: Farrar, Straus, Giroux, 1980).

Chapter 1

1 Cited in Karl Dietrich Bracher, *The German Dictatorship: The Origins, Structure, and Consequences of National Socialism*, trans. Jean Steinberg (Harmondsworth: Penguin, 1970), p. 23.

2 Herbert Marcuse, 'The Struggle against Liberalism in the Totalitarian View of the State' (1934), in *Negations*, trans. Jeremy J. Shapiro (Harmondsworth: Penguin, 1968), p. 3. H. Stuart Hughes, *Consciousness and Society: The Reorientation of European Social Thought, 1890–1930* (Brighton: Harvester Press, 1979), ch. 2. Compare Zeev Sternhell, 'Fascist Ideology', in Walter Laqueur (ed.), *Fascism: A Readers' Guide* (Harmondsworth: Penguin, 1979), p. 333: 'the growth of fascism . . . cannot be understood, or fully explained, unless it is seen in the intellectual, moral, and cultural context which prevailed in Europe at the end of the nineteenth century'. Some fascist philosophers also regard fascism in this way – see Giovanni Gentile, 'The Philosophic Basis of Fascism', *Foreign Affairs*, 6, 1928, pp. 290–304.

3 I have adopted the term 'fascicization' from Zeev Sternhell, *Neither Right Nor Left: Fascist Ideology in France*, trans. David Maisel (Berkeley: University of California Press, 1986), Preface.

4 Friedrich Nietzsche, *Thus Spoke Zarathustra*, trans. R.J. Hollingdale (Harmondsworth: Penguin, 1969), p. 137. For fascist appropriations of Nietzsche, see Alfred Baeumler, 'Nietzsche and National Socialism' (1937), in George Mosse (ed.), *Nazi Culture* (London: W.H. Allen, 1966); and more recently, Bruno Luedtke, 'Nietzsche and National Socialism: Letters to an American Friend', *National Socialist*, no. 1, 1980 and no. 2, 1980.

5 See Henri Bergson, *Matter and Memory* (1986), trans. Nancy Margaret Paul and W. Scott Palmer (London: Macmillan, 1912), and *Creative Evolution* (1907), trans. Arthur Mitchell (London: Macmillan, 1960).

6 See Fritz Stern, *The Politics of Cultural Despair: A Study in the Rise of the Germanic Ideology* (New York: Anchor Books, 1965).

7 His most famous work is *The Psychology of the Crowd* (1895), available as *The Crowd* (New Brunswick, NJ: Transaction Publishers, 1995).

8 Frankfurt Institute for Social Research, *Aspects of Sociology* (1956), trans. John Viertel (London: Heinemann, 1973), p. 76.

9 Le Bon, *The Crowd*, pp. 71, 75, 132.

10 Robert Michels, *Political Parties: A Sociological Study of the Oligarchical Tendencies of Modern Democracy* (1911), trans. Eden and Cedar Paul (New York: Free Press, 1962). See also David Beetham, 'From Socialism to Fascism: The Relation between Theory and Practice in the Work of Robert Michels', *Political Studies*, vol. XXV, nos 1 and 2, 1977.

11 Vilfredo Pareto, *Sociological Writings*, trans. Derick Mirfin, (London:

Pall Mall Press, 1966), pp. 124, 149. See also John Carroll, 'Pareto's Irrationalism', *Sociology*, vol. 7, no. 3, 1973, pp. 327–40.

12 Pierre Drieu La Rochelle, for example, claims that 'certain elements of a fascist atmosphere came together in France around 1913, before they did elsewhere' – cited by Sternhell, *Neither Right Nor Left*, p. 7.

13 Cited in Zeev Sternhell, with Mario Sznajder ànd Maia Asheri, *The Birth of Fascist Ideology*, trans. David Maisel (Princeton, NJ: Princeton University Press, 1994), p. 39.

14 Georges Sorel, 'The Decomposition of Marxism' (1908), in Irving Louis Horowitz, *Radicalism and the Revolt against Reason: The Social Theories of Georges Sorel* (Carbondale and Edwardsville: Southern Illinois University Press, 1968), p. 249. Lawrence Wilde, 'Sorel and the French Right', *History of Political Thought*, vol. VII, no. 2, 1986, p. 370.

15 Sorel considered Le Bon's *Psychology of Socialism* (1898) as the 'most complete work published in France on socialism' – cited in Robert A. Nye, 'Two Paths to a Psychology of Social Action: Gustave Le Bon and Georges Sorel', *Journal of Modern History*, vol. 45, no. 3, 1973, p. 427.

16 Sorel, 'Decomposition of Marxism', p. 248.

17 Georges Sorel, *Reflections on Violence* (1906–8), trans. T.E. Hulme (London: George Allen & Unwin, 1915), pp. 130–1, emphasis added.

18 Ibid., p. 137.

19 Antonio Gramsci, *Selections from the Prison Notebooks*, ed. & trans. Quintin Hoare and Geoffrey Nowell Smith (London: Lawrence & Wishart, 1971), p. 127.

20 Henrik de Man, 'The Psychology of Socialism' (1926), in Peter Dodge (ed.) *A Documentary Study of Henrik de Man, Socialist Critic of Marxism* (Princeton, NJ: Princeton University Press, 1979), pp. 140–1. Also 'The Crisis of Socialism' (1927), in ibid., p. 162.

21 De Man, 'The Psychology of Socialism', pp. 147–8, emphasis added.

22 Henrik de Man, 'The Socialist Idea' (1933), in Dodge, *Documentary Study of Henrik de Man*, pp. 286–7.

23 Sternhell, *Neither Right Nor Left*, pp. 133–4.

24 George Valois, *Le Fascisme*, cited in Sternhell, *Neither Left Nor Right*, p. 9, who also (pp. 21–2) reports the exchange of letters of July and August 1930 between Mussolini and de Man. See also J.L. Talmon, *The Myth of the Nation and the Vision of Revolution* (London: Secker & Warburg, 1981), p. 451.

25 Jean-Paul Sartre, 'Preface' to Frantz Fanon, *The Wretched of the Earth* (New York: Grove Press, 1963), p. 14. The English translation renders *bavardages* as 'utterances' – see Alice Yaeger Kaplan, *Reproductions of Banality: Fascism, Literature, and French Intellectual Life* (Minneapolis: University of Minnesota Press, 1986), ch. 3. For a critique of Sorel along these lines see Wilde, 'Sorel and the French Right'; and

Herbert Marcuse, 'A Study on Authority' (1936), *From Luther to Popper*, trans. Joris De Bres (London: Verso, 1983).

26 As examples, see A. James Gregor, *Young Mussolini and the Intellectual Origins of Fascism* (Berkeley: University of California Press, 1979), p. xi, and Noël O'Sullivan, *Fascism* (London: J.M. Dent, 1983). Liah Greenfeld, *Nationalism: Five Roads to Modernity* (Cambridge, MA: Harvard University Press, 1992), treats Nazism and Marxism as elaborations of the matrix of German nationalism (p. 387).

27 See, for example, his comments in Emil Ludwig, *Talks with Mussolini*, trans. Eden and Cedar Paul (Boston: Little, Brown & Co., 1933), pp. 62, 120, where, among other things, he compares the crowd to a woman in its suggestiveness and simultaneous love and fear of strong men.

28 Ernst Nolte, *Three Faces of Fascism: Action Française, Italian Fascism, National Socialism* (New York: Mentor, 1969), pp. 213, 246.

29 Benito Mussolini, 'Which Way Is the World Going?' (1922), in Adrian Lyttelton (ed.), *Italian Fascisms: From Pareto to Gentile* (London: Jonathan Cape, 1973), pp. 59–67.

30 Benito Mussolini, 'The Doctrine of Fascism' (1932), in Lyttelton, *Italian Fascisms*, p. 56. It also appears to be the case that Mussolini's first use of the phrase 'totalitarian' to describe fascism (on 5 January 1925) was in relation to the will – the will of the great leader would bring about a total transformation. See also Roger Eatwell, *Fascism: A History* (London: Chatto & Windus, 1995), p. 57.

31 Adolf Hitler, *Mein Kampf* (1925), trans. Ralph Manheim (Boston: Houghton Mifflin Company, 1943), p. 332.

32 Cited in J.P. Stern, *Hitler: The Führer and the People* (London: Fontana, 1984), p. 69; also see pp. 56–7.

33 Mussolini, 'Doctrine of Fascism', p. 40.

34 Maurice Barrès, 'Scènes et Doctrines du Nationalisme' (1925), in J.S. McClelland (ed.), *The French Right from de Maistre to Maurras* (London: Jonathan Cape, 1970), pp. 175, 177, 178. Gottfried Benn is cited in Hugh Ridley, 'Irrationalism, Art and Violence: Ernst Jünger and Gottfried Benn', in Alan Bance (ed.), *Weimar Germany: Writers and Politics* (Edinburgh: Scottish Academic Press, 1982), p. 32. Giovanni Gentile, 'The Origins and Doctrine of Fascism' (1934), in Lyttelton, *Italian Fascisms*, pp. 302–6.

35 Mussolini, 'Doctrine of Fascism', pp. 39–44.

36 Hitler, *Mein Kampf*, p. 380. Alfred Rosenberg, *The Myth of the Twentieth Century* (1930) in *Selected Writings*, ed. Robert Pois (London: Jonathan Cape, 1970), p. 84.

37 See Emilio Gentile, 'Fascism as Political Religion', *Journal of Contemporary History* vol. 25, 1990, pp. 229–51; and Robert A. Pois, *National Socialism and the Religion of Nature* (London: Croom Helm, 1986). Gentile in particular draws some useful parallels with the Catholic

Church and Christian organizations generally. For example, the comment by Carlo Scorza, commandant of the fascist youth and the last Partito Nationale Fascista (PNF) secretary, that the party had to develop into more and more of an 'armed religious order' along the lines of the Society of Jesus. Similarly, the new national headquarters of the PNF in 1930 was to embody 'the incomparable energy furnished by the nation's soul', to be 'the temple where new fascist youth will be forged', to have a 'vestry for party banners' and a 'shrine for the martyrs of the fascist revolution'. Pois's focus is on the religion of nature, an issue I take up in Chapter 5.

38 Walter Benjamin, 'Theories of German Fascism: On the Collection of Essays *War and Warrior*, edited by Ernst Jünger' (1930), *New German Critique*, 17, 1979, p. 127.
39 Speech of 22 August 1939, cited in Nolte, *Three Faces of Fascism*, p. 443; see also p. 516.
40 Filippo Marinetti, 'The Founding and Manifesto of Futurism' (1909), in R.W. Flint (ed.), *Marinetti: Selected Writings* (London: Secker & Warburg, 1971), p. 41.
41 Mussolini, 'Doctrine of Fascism', p. 47.
42 Friedrich Nietzsche, 'The Greek State' (1871), in *On the Genealogy of Morals*, trans. Carol Diethe (Cambridge: Cambridge University Press, 1994), pp. 183–5. Joseph de Maistre, *St Petersburg Dialogues, Or Conversations on the Temporal Government of Providence* (1821), trans. Richard A. Lebrun (Montreal: McGill-Queens University Press, 1993), p. 218.
43 See Sternhell, *Neither Right Nor Left*, pp. 55–7, 86–9; and *Birth of Fascist Ideology*, p. 126.
44 O'Sullivan, *Fascism*, p. 72.
45 Gabriele D'Annunzio, 'Letter to the Dalmatians, January 15th, 1919', in Lyttelton, *Italian Fascisms*, p. 185.
46 Ernst Jünger, 'Total Mobilization' (1930), in Richard Wolin (ed.), *The Heidegger Controversy: A Critical Reader* (Cambridge MA: MIT Press, 1993), p. 123; see also Jünger, 'On Danger' (1931), *New German Critique*, 59, 1993, pp. 27–32.
47 Hitler, *Mein Kampf*, p. 177. Valois is cited in Talmon, *Myth of the Nation*, p. 473. Maurras is cited in Nolte, *Three Faces of Fascism*, p. 155.
48 Benjamin, 'Theories of German Fascism', pp. 121–2; see also Benjamin 'The Work of Art in the Age of Mechanical Reproduction', in Benjamin, *Illuminations*, trans. Harry Zohn (London: Fontana, 1970).
49 See Mark Neocleous, 'Perpetual War, Or, "War and War Again": Schmitt, Foucault, Fascism', *Philosophy and Social Criticism*, vol. 22, no. 2, 1996, pp. 47–66.
50 A formulation I am borrowing from Greil Marcus, *Lipstick Traces: A*

Secret History of the Twentieth Century (London: Secker & Warburg, 1989), p. 431.

51 Benito Mussolini, 'Trenchocracy' (1917), in Roger Griffin (ed.), *Fascism* (Oxford: Oxford University Press, 1995), pp. 28–9. On the cult of the fallen soldier, see George Mosse, *Fallen Soldiers: Reshaping the Memories of the World Wars* (Oxford: Oxford University Press, 1990). The new 'ism' which came into use in 1920 was, significantly, the product of the *Fasci di combattimento* – bundles of fighters. And as George Mosse notes in *Nationalism and Sexuality: Middle-Class Morality and Sexual Norms in Modern Europe* (Madison: University of Wisconsin Press, 1985), p. 154, fascism's ideal type of community is rooted in the military form – historically, the storm-trooper in Germany or the *arditi* in Italy. These are, of course, communities of men, a point we shall return to in Chapter 5.

52 Ansgar Hillach, 'The Aesthetics of Politics: Walter Benjamin's "Theories of German Fascism"'', *New German Critique*, 17, p. 106.

Chapter 2

1 Benito Mussolini, 'The Naples Speech' (1922), in Roger Griffen (ed.), *Fascism* (Oxford: Oxford University Press, 1995), pp. 43–4. Ernst Nolte, *Three Faces of Fascism: Action Française, Italian Fascism, National Socialism* (New York: Mentor, 1969), p. 201.

2 Emil Ludwig, *Talks with Mussolini*, trans. Eden and Cedar Paul (Boston: Little, Brown and Co., 1933), p. 145.

3 Mussolini, 'Naples Speech', emphasis added.

4 A. James Gregor, *Young Mussolini and the Intellectual Origins of Fascism* (Berkeley: University of California Press, 1979), p. 75. Compare Gregor, *The Fascist Persuasion in Radical Politics* (Princeton, NJ: Princeton University Press, 1974), p. 170.

5 See, for example, Enrico Corradini, 'The Proletarian Nations and Nationalism' (1911) and 'Nationalism and Democracy' (1913), in Adrian Lyttelton (ed.), *Italian Fascisms: From Pareto to Gentile* (London: Jonathan Cape, 1973), pp. 149–51, 152–4.

6 Adolf Hitler, *Mein Kampf* (1925), trans. Ralph Manheim (Boston: Houghton Mifflin Company, 1943), pp. 333–43. See also George Mosse, *The Nationalization of the Masses: Political Symbolism and Mass Movements in Germany from the Napoleonic Wars through the Third Reich* (New York: Howard Fertig, 1975), ch. 8.

7 Ibid., p. 10; see also p. 13.

8 Tom Nairn, *The Break-up of Britain: Crisis and Neo-Nationalism*, 2nd edn (London: Verso, 1981), p. 347.

9 See especially Zeev Sternhell, 'Fascist Ideology', in Walter Laqueur (ed.), *Fascism: A Reader's Guide* (Harmondsworth: Penguin, 1979);

Sternhell, with Mario Sznajder and Maia Asheri, *The Birth of Fascist Ideology*, trans. David Maisel (Princeton, NJ: Princeton University Press, 1994); Karl Dietrich Bracher, 'The Role of Hitler: Perspectives of Interpretation' in Laqueur, *Fascism*; Bracher, *The Age of Ideologies: A History of Political Thought in the Twentieth Century*, trans. Ewald Osers (London: Methuen, 1985), p. 82; Gilbert Allardyce, 'What Fascism Is Not: Thoughts on the Deflation of a Concept', *American Historical Review*, vol. 84, no. 2, 1979, pp. 367–88. Despite recognizing the 'red herring' of racism, Eugen Weber, in *Varieties of Fascism: Doctrines of Revolution in the Twentieth Century* (Princeton, New Jersey: Anvil, 1964), nevertheless also separates it from fascism. Other reasons are sometimes given as to why a concept of generic fascism is impossible, concerning modernity and tradition. This is dealt with in Chapter 4.

10 Tim Mason, 'Whatever Happened to "Fascism"?', in Jane Caplan (ed.) *Nazism, Fascism and the Working Class: Essays by Tim Mason* (Cambridge: Cambridge University Press, 1995), p. 325. Compare Allardyce, 'What Fascism Is Not', p. 383: 'Auschwitz is the riddle of fascism studies'.

11 J.L. Talmon, *The Myth of the Nation and the Vision of Revolution* (London: Secker & Warburg, 1981), p. 476.

12 Benito Mussolini, 'The Doctrine of Fascism', in Lyttelton, *Italian Fascisms*, p. 43. Giovanni Gentile, 'The Philosophic Basis of Fascism', *Foreign Affairs*, 6, 1928, p. 294.

13 Mussolini, 'Doctrine of Fascism', pp. 42–3.

14 Hitler, *Mein Kampf*, pp. 95–6, 386, 391–4.

15 Alfred Rosenberg, 'Totaler Staat?' (1934), in Robert Pois (ed.) *Alfred Rosenberg: Selected Writings* (London: Jonathan Cape, 1970), pp. 191–2.

16 Roger Griffin, *The Nature of Fascism* (London: Routledge, 1993), p. 85.

17 Mosse, *The Crisis of German Ideology: Intellectual Origins of the Third Reich* (London: Weidenfeld & Nicolson, 1966), p. 15; also p. 9. Also see Mosse 'Fascism and the Intellectuals' in S.J. Woolf (ed.), *The Nature of Fascism* (London: Weidenfeld & Nicolson, 1968), p. 216; Hermann Glaser, *The Cultural Roots of National Socialism*, trans. Ernest A. Menze (London: Croom Helm, 1978); Daniel Jonah Goldhagen, *Hitler's Willing Executioners: Ordinary Germans and the Holocaust* (London: Little, Brown and Co., 1996), pp. 74, 77, and ch. 3 in particular.

18 Fritz Stern, *The Politics of Cultural Despair: A Study in the Rise of the Germanic Ideology* (New York: Doubleday & Co., 1965). See also Mosse, *Crisis of German Ideology*.

19 Anton Kaes, Martin Jay and Edward Dimendberg (eds), *The Weimar*

Republic Sourcebook (Berkeley: University of California Press, 1994), p. 330.

20 Peter Gay, *The Cultivation of Hatred: The Bourgeois Experience, Victoria to Freud, Vol. III* (London: HarperCollins, 1994), pp. 73–5, 82–3.

21 Tzvetan Todorov, *On Human Diversity: Nationalism, Racism, and Exoticism in French Thought*, trans. Catherine Porter (Cambridge, MA: Harvard University Press, 1993), p. 90.

22 Hitler, *Mein Kampf*, pp. 362–3, 378–85, 460–1.

23 Geoff Eley, *Reshaping the German Right: Radical Nationalism and Political Change after Bismarck* (Ann Arbor: University of Michigan Press, 1991), pp. 185–6.

24 On Gobineau, see Michael D. Biddiss (ed.) *Gobineau: Selected Writings* (London: Jonathan Cape, 1970); and Biddiss, *Father of Racist Ideology: The Social and Political Thought of Count Gobineau* (London: Weidenfeld & Nicolson, 1970). For Chamberlain, see Roderick Stackelberg, *Idealism Debased: From Völkisch Ideology to National Socialism* (Kent, OH: Kent State University Press, 1981), Part Three.

25 Moreover, in his attempt to present European racism as leading to the final solution, Mosse obliterates the national context in which writers such as Benedict Morel in France and Cesar Lombroso in Italy worked. And in his concern to point out the continued dangers of such thinking, Mosse himself moves from the German context and points to the way in which American groups who 'want to segregate Negro from white . . . embrace the volkish ideology' without justifying this leap or sensing any difficulties in doing so. See George Mosse, *Toward the Final Solution: A History of European Racism* (London: Dent & Sons, 1978), pp. 82–3; Mosse, *Crisis of German Ideology*, p. 10.

26 For a general account of the problems of focusing on 'German peculiarity' see David Blackbourn and Geoff Eley, *The Peculiarities of German History: Bourgeois Society and Politics in Nineteenth-Century Germany* (Oxford: Oxford University Press, 1984). For a wider discussion in the context of state and class in Britain, see Mark Neocleous, *Administering Civil Society: Towards a Theory of State Power* (London: Macmillan, 1996), ch. 4.

27 The Programme is reprinted in J. Noakes and G. Pridham (eds), *Nazism 1919–1945, Vol. 1: The Rise to Power 1919–1934* (Exeter: University of Exeter, 1983), pp. 14–16.

28 In 1923; cited in Anna Bramwell, *Blood and Soil: Walther Darré and Hitler's 'Green Party'* (Bourne End: Kensal Press, 1985), p. 36.

29 Hitler, *Mein Kampf*, pp. 290–3, 389, 392, 395, 403–7, 442.

30 Hitler, interview with the *New York Times*, 10 July 1933, cited in Alan Bullock, 'The Political Ideas of Adolf Hitler', in International Council

for Philosophy and Humanistic Studies, *The Third Reich* (London: Weidenfeld & Nicolson, 1955), p. 362.

31 See the 'Program' of the DNVP from 1931 reprinted in Kaes *et al.*, *Weimar Republic Sourcebook*, pp. 348–52. For Moeller van den Bruck, see Kaes *et al.*, *Weimar Republic Sourcebook*, pp. 332–4, and Stern, *Politics of Cultural Despair*, Part III.

32 Maurice Barrès, 'Scènes et Doctrines du Nationalisme' (1925), in J.S. McClelland (ed.), *The French Right from de Maistre to Maurras* (London: Jonathan Cape, 1970), pp. 159, 162, 184.

33 Todorov, *On Human Diversity*, pp. 230, 248.

34 Hitler, *Mein Kampf*, pp. 327, 339, 393.

35 Ibid., pp. 231–3, 243, 304, 337. See also Chapter 5 of this book.

36 Ernst Bloch, *Heritage of Our Times*, trans. Neville and Stephen Plaice (Cambridge: Polity, 1991), pp. 91–2.

37 Hitler, *Mein Kampf*, pp. 150, 303–5, 623. Hitler was still thinking of the Jews in this way in 1945. See François Genoud (ed.), *The Testament of Adolf Hitler: The Hitler-Bormann Documents, February–April 1945*, trans. Colonel R. Stevens (London: Icon Books, 1962), p. 60. Hannah Arendt, *The Origins of Totalitarianism* (San Diego, CA: Harcourt Brace and Co. 1973), chs 2 and 3; see also the appropriation and reworking of her account by Zygmunt Bauman, *Modernity and the Holocaust* (Cambridge: Polity Press, 1989).

38 Bauman, *Modernity and the Holocaust*, p. 55.

39 Peter Pulzer, *The Rise of Political Anti-Semitism in Germany and Austria* (London: Peter Halban, 1988), p. 221. My intention here is thus diametrically opposed to that of those who seek to separate nationalism from fascism – see, for example, Anthony D. Smith, *Theories of Nationalism*, 2nd edn (London: Duckworth, 1983), Appendix B – and those who seek to salvage some kind of civic nationalism from the wreckage brought about by the history of nationalism in the twentieth century – see, for example, Michael Ignatieff, *Blood and Belonging: Journeys into the New Nationalism* (London: Vintage, 1994).

40 Arendt, *Origins of Totalitarianism*, p. 5.

41 'Manifesto of the NSDAP, 1930', in Noakes and Pridham (eds), *Nazism 1919–1945, Vol. I*, p. 72.

42 See Theodore Abel, *Why Hitler Came to Power* (Cambridge, MA: Harvard University Press, 1986), first published in 1938; Peter H. Merkl, *Political Violence Under the Swastika: 581 Early Nazis* (Princeton, NJ: Princeton University Press, 1975), pp. 453, 498–507; John Hiden and John Farquharson, *Explaining Hitler's Germany: Historians and the Third Reich* (London: Batsford, 1983), pp. 41–4.

43 Arno J. Mayer, *Why Did the Heavens Not Darken?: The 'Final Solution' in History* (London: Verso, 1990), p. 108. Henry Ashby Turner points out that Hitler 'soft-pedaled or left altogether unmentioned his

anti-Semitism when speaking to men of big business, having recognized its unpopularity in those circles' – *German Big Business and the Rise of Hitler* (Oxford: Oxford University Press, 1985), pp. 343 and 348.

44 See my comments on this in the Conclusion.

45 Cited by Ludwig, *Talks with Mussolini*, pp. 69–70.

46 Mosse, *Toward the Final Solution*, pp. 200, 230.

47 Luigi Preti, 'Fascist Imperialism and Racism', in Roland Sarti (ed.), *The Ax Within: Italian Fascism in Action* (New York: New Viewpoints, 1974). The account of Mussolini's racism and anti-Semitism has been adopted from Preti's article and Denis Mack Smith, *Mussolini* (St Albans: Granada, 1983), pp. 256–8.

48 A. James Gregor, *The Ideology of Fascism: The Rationale of Totalitarianism* (New York: Free Press, 1969), pp. 246–7, from where the citations from Mussolini's speech are taken.

49 Ibid., pp. 248, 256.

50 Mussolini, June 1919, cited in Gregor, *Ideology of Fascism*, p. 250.

51 The 1938 *Manifesto of Fascist Racism* is indicative of the ambiguities concerning 'race' and the pretence that it can be non-biological. The document concedes that 'the concept of race is a concept essentially biological', but also denies that fascist racism is the same as 'German' racism. A *purely* biological concept of race would mean undermining the concept of the nation – for races would then be conceived of like classes in Marxism, as transcending and thus threatening national boundaries. But when the *Manifesto* tries to rework the biology of race through the idea of population and history it is still reduced to talking about the pure 'Italian race' rooted in the blood of Italian families. The Manifesto is reproduced as 'Appendix A' of Gregor, *Ideology of Fascism*. In that book (pp. 265–82) Gregor gives a good account of the Manifesto's complexities, including Mussolini's description of the *Manifesto* as a German text translated into bad Italian (p. 277).

52 Benedict Anderson, *Imagined Communities: Reflections on the Origin and Spread of Nationalism*, revised edn (London: Verso, 1991), p. 149.

53 Nairn, *Break-up of Britain*, p. 41.

Chapter 3

1 Russell Berman, *Modern Culture and Critical Theory: Art, Politics, and the Legacy of the Frankfurt School* (Madison: University of Wisconsin Press, 1989), p. 99.

2 A. James Gregor, *The Fascist Persuasion in Radical Politics* (Princeton, NJ: Princeton University Press, 1974); Gregor, *Young Mussolini and the Intellectual Origins of Fascism* (Berkeley: University of California Press, 1979); Noël O'Sullivan, *Fascism* (London: J.M. Dent & Sons, 1983); Zeev Sternhell, with Mario Sznajder and Maia Asheri, *The Birth*

of Fascist Ideology: From Cultural Rebellion to Political Revolution, trans. David Maisel (Princeton, NJ: Princeton University Press, 1994).

3 George Valois, 'Empty Portfolios' (1926), in Roger Griffen (ed.), *Fascism* (Oxford: Oxford University Press, 1995), pp. 197–8; Zeev Sternhell, *Neither Right Nor Left: Fascist Ideology in France*, trans. David Maisel (Berkeley: University of California Press, 1986), pp. 105–6. On Drieu and Barrès, see Robert Soucy, *Fascist Intellectual: Drieu La Rochelle* (Berkeley: University of California Press, 1979), and *Fascism in France: The Case of Maurice Barrès* (Berkeley: University of California Press, 1972).

4 Adolf Hitler, *Mein Kampf* (1925), trans. Ralph Manheim (Boston: Houghton Miffin Co., 1943), pp. 155, 168, 209, 333, 336, 427, 600–1, 679.

5 Herbert Marcuse, 'The Struggle against Liberalism in the Totalitarian View of the State' (1934), in *Negations: Essays in Critical Theory*, trans. Jeremy Shapiro (Harmondsworth: Penguin, 1968), p. 21. Max Horkheimer, 'The Jews and Europe', in Stephen Eric Bronner and Douglas MacKay Kellner (eds), *Critical Theory and Society: A Reader* (London: Routledge, 1989), p. 85.

6 See Karl Marx and Frederick Engels, *The German Ideology*, ed. Chris Arthur (London: Lawrence and Wishart, 1970), p. 41.

7 Hitler, Speech in December 1930, cited in Tim Mason, *Social Policy in the Third Reich: The Working Class and the 'National Community'*, trans. John Broadwin (Oxford: Berg, 1993), p. 25.

8 Franz Neumann, *Behemoth: The Structure and Practice of National Socialism* (London: Victor Gollancz, 1942), p. 107. Ernst Bloch, *Heritage of Our Times*, trans. Neville and Stephen Plaice (Cambridge: Polity, 1991), p. 44.

9 See George Mosse, *The Crisis of German Ideology: Intellectual Origins of the Third Reich* (London: Weidenfeld & Nicolson, 1966), pp. 21–2.

10 Benito Mussolini, 'The Doctrine of Fascism', in Adrian Lyttelton (ed.), *Italian Fascisms: From Pareto to Gentile* (London: Jonathan Cape, 1973), p. 42. Giovanni Gentile, 'The Philosophic Basis of Fascism', *Foreign Affairs*, vol. 6, 1928, pp. 290–304, claims that corporatism is expected to unite as a productive force the whole of society. Ernst Nolte, *Three Faces of Fascism: Action Française, Italian Fascism, National Socialism*, trans. Leila Vennewitz (New York: Mentor, 1969), p. 264.

11 Robert Soucy, *French Fascism: The First Wave, 1924–1933* (New Haven, CT: Yale University Press, 1986), p. 160.

12 Nolte, *Three Faces of Fascism*, p. 269; George Mosse, 'Mass Politics and the Political Liturgy of Nationalism', in Eugene Kamenka (ed.), *Nationalism: The Nature and Evolution of an Idea* (London: Edward Arnold, 1976), p. 40.

13 Walter Benjamin, 'The Work of Art in the Age of Mechanical Reproduction', in Benjamin, *Illuminations*, trans. Harry Zohn (London: Fontana, 1973), p. 243.

14 Horkheimer, 'The Jews and Europe', p. 78; Tim Mason, 'Open Questions on Fascism', in Raphael Samuel (ed.), *People's History and Socialist Theory* (London: Routledge, 1981), p. 205.

15 See David Blackbourn and Geoff Eley, *The Peculiarities of German History: Bourgeois Society and Politics in Nineteenth-Century Germany* (Oxford: Oxford University Press, 1984), p. 26.

16 Sergei Eisenstein, 'On Fascism, German Cinema and Real Life. Open Letter to the German Minister of Propaganda, Dr Goebbels', in Richard Taylor (ed. and trans.) *Sergei Eisenstein: Selected Works Vol. I, Writings 1922–1934* (London: British Film Institute, 1988), p. 283.

17 Neumann, *Behemoth*, p. 264: 'whenever the outcry against the sovereignty of banking capital is injected into a popular movement, it is the surest sign that fascism is on its way'.

18 After the First World War the *Popolo d'Italia* was given the new subtitle 'The Newspaper of Combatants and Producers'; its previous subtitle had been 'Socialist Daily'. Mussolini, 'Doctrine of Fascism', p. 45.

19 From *The Fascist Era*, published by the CGII in 1939, cited in Hannah Arendt, *The Origins of Totalitarianism* (New York: Harcourt Brace & Co., 1973), p. 258n.

20 Roland Sarti, *Fascism and the Industrial Leadership in Italy, 1919–1940: A Study of the Expansion of Private Power under Fascism* (Los Angeles: University of California Press, 1971), p. 76.

21 Goebbels, *Der Nazi-Sozi* (1931), cited in Daniel Guerin, *Fascism and Big Business* (New York: Pathfinder Press, 1973), p. 81. Hitler, *Mein Kampf*, pp. 51, 63, 65, 323.

22 Henry Friedlander, 'The Manipulation of Language', in Henry Friedlander and Sybil Milton (eds), *The Holocaust: Ideology, Bureaucracy and Genocide* (New York: Krause International Publications, 1980), p. 105.

23 Neumann, *Behemoth*, p. 337. Martin Broszat, *The Hitler State: The Foundation and Development of the Internal Structure of the Third Reich*, trans. John Hiden (Harlow: Longman, 1981), p. 139.

24 Hitler, *Mein Kampf*, pp. 323, 339. He adds that trade unions are in fact crucial for national life, but they need to become national socialist and thus relinquish their role as organs of class struggle imposed on them by Marxists (pp. 598–600). John Hiden and John Farquharson, *Explaining Hitler's Germany: Historians and the Third Reich* (London: Batsford, 1983), p. 103.

25 Joan Campbell, *Joy in Work, German Work: The National Debate, 1800–1945* (Princeton, NJ: Princeton University Press, 1989), pp. 321–4.

26 Neumann, *Behemoth*, pp. 187, 338, 340; Broszat, *The Hitler State*, pp. 145–6; Tim Mason, 'The Law on the Organization of National Labour of 20 January 1934. An Investigation into the Relationship between "Archaic" and "Modern" Elements in Recent German History', in Jane Caplan (ed.) *Nazism, Fascism and the Working Class: Essays by Tim Mason* (Cambridge: Cambridge University Press, 1995), pp. 80–2; and Mason, *Social Policy in the Third Reich*, pp. 104, 164.

27 Tim Mason, 'The Containment of the Working Class in Nazi Germany', in Caplan, *Nazism, Fascism and the Working Class*, p. 239. Bloch, *Heritage of Our Times*, pp. 64–8, 117–8, 141.

28 Campbell, *Joy in Work*, pp. 352, 357; Friedlander, 'Manipulation of Language', p. 106.

29 Klaus Theweleit, *Male Fantasies, Vol. 2: Male Bodies: Psychoanalyzing the White Terror*, trans. Chris Turner and Erica Carter (Cambridge: Polity Press, 1989), p. 87.

30 Tim Mason, 'Labour in the Third Reich, 1933–1939', *Past and Present*, 33, 1966, p. 120.

31 Anson Rabinbach, 'The Aesthetics of Production in the Third Reich', *Journal of Contemporary History*, 11, 1976, p. 50.

32 Mark Prendergast, *For God, Country and Coca-Cola: The Unauthorized History of the World's Most Popular Soft Drink* (London: Weidenfeld & Nicolson, 1993), ch. 13: 'Coca-Cola Über Alles'.

33 Eric Hobsbawm, *Age of Extremes: The Short Twentieth Century, 1914–1991* (Harmondsworth: Penguin, 1994), p. 129. Neumann, *Behemoth*, p. 182.

34 See Turner, *German Big Business and the Rise of Hitler* (Oxford: Oxford University Press, 1985), p. 358: 'He [Horkheimer] and the others who had applied that formula had been mistaken about the nature of Nazism at the time, but most learned nothing from their defeat. Nor have their disciples, who continue to subordinate the study of Nazism to a crusade against capitalism'.

35 Arthur Moeller van den Bruck, 'The Third Empire', in Anton Kaes, Martin Jay and Edward Dimendberg (eds), *The Weimar Republic Sourcebook* (Berkeley, CA: University of California Press, 1994), pp. 332–4; Fritz Stern, *The Politics of Cultural Despair: A Study in the Rise of the Germanic Ideology* (New York: Doubleday & Co., 1965), pp. 275, 313.

36 See Gentile, 'Philosophic Basis of Fascism', p. 299.

37 See, for example, Alfred Rosenberg, 'Totaler Staat?' (1934), in Robert Pois (ed.) *Alfred Rosenberg: Selected Writings* (London: Jonathan Cape, 1970), p. 191; Adolf Hitler, 'The National Socialist Revolution' (30 January 1937), in Bruce Mazlish, Arthur D. Kaledin and David B. Ralston (eds), *Revolution: A Reader* (New York: Macmillan, 1971), pp. 470–85. See Hans Mommsen, *From Weimar to Auschwitz: Essays in*

German History, trans. Philip O'Connor (Cambridge: Polity Press, 1991), p. 152, for similar comments by Goebbels.

38 Hermann Rauschning, *The Revolution of Nihilism: Warning to the West*, trans. E.W. Dickes (New York: Alliance Book Corporation, 1939). On Germany in particular, see David Schoenbaum, *Hitler's Social Revolution: Class and Status in Nazi Germany 1933–1939* (London: Weidenfeld & Nicolson, 1967); Ralf Dahrendorf, *Society and Democracy in Germany* (London: Weidenfeld & Nicolson, 1967), pp. 402–18; and Daniel Jonah Goldhagen, *Hitler's Willing Executioners: Ordinary Germans and the Holocaust* (London: Little, Brown and Co., 1996), pp. 173, 455–63. On revolution and fascism generally, see O'Sullivan, *Fascism*, p. 39; Roger Griffen, *The Nature of Fascism* (London: Routledge, 1993), p. 48; George Mosse, 'Introduction: Towards a General Theory of Fascism', in Mosse (ed.), *International Fascism: New Thoughts and New Approaches* (London: Sage, 1979), pp. 5, 36.

39 Jeremy Noakes, 'Nazism and Revolution', in Noel O'Sullivan (ed.), *Revolutionary Theory and Political Reality* (Brighton: Wheatsheaf, 1983), p. 73; Ian Kershaw, *The Nazi Dictatorship: Problems and Perspectives of Interpretation*, 2nd edn. (London: Edward Arnold, 1989), p. 132.

40 Cited in Neumann, *Behemoth*, p. 378, from Mussolini's 'Relativismo e Fascismo', emphasis added. Mussolini goes on to add that 'it is sufficient to have a single fixed point: the nation'. See also Mussolini, 'Doctrine of Fascism', pp. 40, 42.

41 See, for example, Eugen Weber, 'Revolution? Counter-Revolution? What Revolution?' in Laqueur (ed.), *Fascism: A Reader's Guide* (Harmondsworth: Penguin, 1979), pp. 488–531.

42 K. Marx, *Contribution to the Critique of Political Economy*, Preface. See also *Capital, Vol. 1*, trans. Ben Fowkes (Harmondsworth: Penguin, 1976), chs 29–31, and 'Conspectus of Bakunin's *Statism and Anarchy*', in David Fernbach (ed.) *The First International and After* (Harmondsworth: Penguin, 1974), p. 334, where Marx castigates Bakunin for understanding nothing of the *social* revolution, only its *political* phrases. For a more comprehensive account and development of this approach, see Mark Neocleous, *Administering Civil Society: Towards a Theory of State Power* (London: Macmillan, 1996), Chapter 4.

43 In Blackbourn and Eley, *Peculiarities of German History*, p. 82; in his essay in the book Blackbourn calls this the silent bourgeois revolution.

44 Neumann, *Behemoth*; Noakes, 'Nazism and Revolution', p. 84; Kershaw, *The Nazi Dictatorship*, p. 143.

45 Hobsbawm, *Age of Extremes*, p. 128.

46 See Mommsen, *From Weimar to Auschwitz*, p. 152. Adrian Lyttelton, 'Fascism in Italy: The Second Wave', in Roland Sarti (ed.), *The Ax*

Within: Italian Fascism in Action (New York: New Viewpoints, 1974), pp. 61, 67. In a speech to the Assembly of the Fascist Party on 28 January, 1924, Mussolini declared that 'The Fascist revolution is not bedecked with human sacrifices; it has not created special tribunals; the rattling of the firing squads has not been heard; terror has not been exercised; emergency laws have not been promulgated' – cited in Lyttelton, n. 2, p. 235.

47 See Arno J. Mayer, *Dynamics of Counterrevolution in Europe, 1870–1956: An Analytic Framework* (New York: Harper Torchbooks, 1971).

48 Cited in Lionel Kochan, *The Struggle for Germany, 1914–1945* (Edinburgh: Edinburgh University Press, 1963), p. 64. Kochan adds that while many nuances of response to Nazism existed, none was such as to go beyond accepting Germany as a partner in the struggle against communism.

49 Hugo von Hofmannsthal, 'Literature as the Spiritual Space of the Nation' (1927), in Kaes *et al.*, *The Weimar Republic Sourcebook*, p. 341.

50 Edgar J. Jung, 'Germany and the Conservative Revolution' (1932) in Kaes *et al.*, *The Weimar Republic Sourcebook*, p. 352. Moeller van den Bruck liked to quote Dostoevsky's claim that 'we are revolutionaries out of conservatism' – cited in Stern, *Politics of Cultural Despair*, p. 261. See also Roy Pascal, 'Revolutionary Conservatism: Moeller van den Bruck', in International Council for Philosophy and Humanistic Studies (ed.), *The Third Reich* (London: Weidenfeld & Nicolson, 1955).

51 Cited in Weber, 'Revolution? Counter-revolution? What Revolution?', p. 523. See also the passages cited in notes 40 and 46 above. For an account of how the work of one conservative revolutionary, Carl Schmitt, is developed partly from an understanding of Italian fascism and then used to legitimize Nazism, see Mark Neocleous, 'Friend or Enemy? Reading Schmitt Politically', *Radical Philosophy*, 79, 1996, pp. 13–23.

52 José Antonio Primo de Rivera, 'On the Occasion of the Foundation of the Spanish Falange', in Hugh Thomas (ed.), *José Antonio Primo de Rivera: Selected Writings* (London: Jonathan Cape, 1972), pp. 53–4.

53 George Mosse, 'Introduction: Towards a General Theory of Fascism', pp. 6–10, 36. Zeev Sternhell, 'Fascist Ideology' in Laqueur, *Fascism*, pp. 377, 393.

Chapter 4

1 Ralf Dahrendorf, *Society and Democracy in Germany* (London: Weidenfeld & Nicolson, 1967), pp. 402–18. Similar claims are made by David Schoenbaum, *Hitler's Social Revolution: Class and Status in Nazi Germany, 1933–39* (London: Weidenfeld & Nicolson, 1967).

2 A. James Gregor, *Italian Fascism and Developmental Dictatorship* (New Jersey: Princeton University Press, 1979). Hans Rogger, 'Afterthoughts', in Hans Rogger and Eugen Weber (eds), *The European Right: A Historical Profile* (London: Weidenfeld & Nicolson, 1965), p. 588. George L. Mosse, *The Crisis of German Ideology: Intellectual Origins of the Third Reich* (London: Weidenfeld & Nicolson, 1964), p. 316. Fritz Stern, *The Politics of Cultural Despair: A Study in the Rise of the Germanic Ideology* (New York: Doubleday and Co., 1965), pp. 4–8. See also Henry Ashby Turner, 'Fascism and Modernization', *World Politics*, 24, 1972, pp. 547–64, where fascism is read as a utopian anti-modernism.

3 Renzo de Felice, *Fascism: An Informal Introduction to Its Theory and Practice. An Interview with Michael Ledeen* (New Brunswick, NJ: Transaction Books, 1976), p. 56. See also A. James Gregor, *The Ideology of Fascism: The Rationale of Totalitarianism* (New York: Free Press, 1969), Preface, who concedes that Nazism does not fit into his concept of fascism as a developmental and thus modernizing dictatorship; and Turner, 'Fascism and Modernization'. On the other hand, contrast Ernst Nolte, *Three Faces of Fascism: Action Française, Italian Fascism, National Socialism*, trans. Leila Vennewitz (New York: Mentor, 1965), p. 467, who claims that whereas the lictor's bundle recalled a remote era, the swastika was supposed to proclaim a future victory.

4 Jeffrey Herf, *Reactionary Modernism: Technology, Culture, and Politics in Weimar and the Third Reich* (Cambridge: Cambridge University Press, 1984).

5 For variations on this problem see ibid., p. 12; Marshall Berman, *All That Is Solid Melts into Air: The Experience of Modernity* (London: Verso, 1983), p. 88; and Alice Yaeger Kaplan, *Reproductions of Banality: Fascism, Literature, and French Intellectual Life* (Minneapolis: University of Minnesota Press, 1986), p. 25.

6 Karl Marx and Friedrich Engels, *The Communist Manifesto* (London: Penguin, 1967), p. 83.

7 For a general account, see Stephen Kern, *The Culture of Time and Space, 1880–1914* (London: Weidenfeld & Nicolson, 1983). For the social and cultural effects of one new form of technology – the machine-gun – on European society, see John Ellis, *The Social History of the Machine Gun* (London: Hutchinson, 1987).

8 R.W. Flint (ed.) *Marinetti: Selected Writings*, (London: Secker & Warburg, 1971). See also Anne Bowler, 'Politics as Art: Italian Futurism and Fascism', *Theory and Society*, vol. 20, no. 6, 1991, pp. 763–94.

9 James Joll, *Three Intellectuals in Politics: Blum, Rathenau, Marinetti* (New York: Harper and Row, 1965), p. 177.

10 Jeffrey T. Schnapp, 'Epic Demonstrations: Fascist Modernity and the 1932 Exhibition of the Fascist Revolution', in Richard J. Goslin (ed.), *Fascism, Aesthetics, and Culture* (Hanover, NH: University Press of New England, 1992), p. 16.

11 George L. Mosse, 'The Political Culture of Italian Futurism: A General Perspective', *Journal of Contemporary History*, 25, 1990, p. 256.

12 Joseph Goebbels, speech at the opening of the Berlin Auto Show, 17 February 1939, cited in Herf, *Reactionary Modernism*, p. 196.

13 Turner, 'Fascism and Modernization', p. 556; Herf, *Reactionary Modernism*, pp. 194–5.

14 Ernst Jünger, *Das Waldchen 125* (1925), cited in Michael E. Zimmerman, *Heidegger's Confrontation with Modernity: Technology, Politics, Art* (Indianapolis: Indiana University Press, 1990), p. 46. See also Jünger 'Total Mobilization' (1930), in Richard Wolin (ed.), *The Heidegger Controversy: A Critical Reader* (Cambridge, MA: MIT Press, 1991); and Jünger, 'On Danger' (1931), *New German Critique*, 59, 1993, pp. 27–32.

15 See Henry Friedlander, 'The Manipulation of Language', in Henry Friedlander and Sybil Milton (eds), *The Holocaust: Ideology, Bureaucracy and Genocide* (New York: Kraus International Publications, 1980), pp. 103–4.

16 E.H. Gombrich, *The Sense of Order: A Study in the Psychology of Decorative Art* (Oxford: Phaidon Press, 1979), p. 138; Siegfried Kracauer, *From Caligari to Hitler: A Psychological History of the German Film* (Princeton, NJ: Princeton University Press, 1947), p. 301; Malcolm Quinn, *The Swastika: Constructing the Symbol* (London: Routledge, 1994), pp. 78–80, 104–5. Compare Wilhelm Reich's presentation of the swastika as an emblem of intercourse, in *The Mass Psychology of Fascism*, trans. Vincent R. Carfagno (Harmondsworth: Penguin, 1970), pp. 131–6.

17 See Charles Maier, *In Search of Stability: Explorations in Historical Political Economy* (Cambridge: Cambridge University Press, 1987), ch. 1. See also Herf, *Reactionary Modernism*, ch. 3.

18 Zygmunt Bauman, *Modernity and the Holocaust* (Cambridge: Polity Press, 1989), pp. 46, 150.

19 Ernst Bloch, *Heritage of Our Times*, trans. Neville and Stephen Plaice (Cambridge: Polity, 1991). Arno J. Mayer, *Why Did the Heavens Not Darken? The 'Final Solution' in History* (London: Verso, 1990), p. 96.

20 Emilio Gentile, 'Fascism as Political Religion', *Journal of Contemporary History*, 25, 1990, p. 244.

21 Mussolini, 21 April 1922, cited in Gentile, 'Fascism as Political Religion', p. 245.

22 Romke Visser, 'Fascist Doctrine and the Cult of the *Romanità*',

Journal of Contemporary History, 27, 1992, pp. 5–22. Roger Eatwell, *Fascism: A History* (London: Chatto & Windus, 1995), pp. 37, 57.

23 See the images collected in Robert S. Wistrich, *Weekend in Munich: Art, Propaganda and Terror in the Third Reich* (London: Pavilion Books, 1995).

24 Bloch, *Heritage of Our Times*, p. 66. See also Franz Neumann, *Behemoth: The Structure and Practice of National Socialism* (London: Victor Gollancz, 1942), pp. 341–4; Robert Koehl, 'Feudal Aspects of National Socialism', *American Political Science Review*, vol. 54, no. 4, 1960, pp. 921–33.

25 Anson Rabinbach, 'The Aesthetics of Production in the Third Reich', *Journal of Contemporary History*, 11, 1976, pp. 43–74; Rabinbach, *The Human Motor: Energy, Fatigue, and the Origins of Modernity* (London: HarperCollins, 1990), pp. 286–7. Peter Labanyi, 'Images of Fascism: Visualization and Aestheticization in the Third Reich', in Michael Laffan (ed.), *The Burden of German History, 1919–45: Essays for the Goethe Institute* (London: Methuen, 1988), p. 167. Quinn, *The Swastika*, Preface.

26 Schnapp, 'Epic Demonstrations', p. 22.

27 Kaplan, *Reproductions of Banality*, p. 32; Herf, *Reactionary Modernism*, p. 24.

28 Tim Mason, 'The Origins of the Law on the Organization of National Labour of 20 January 1934. An Investigation into the Relationship between "Archaic" and "Modern" Elements in Recent German History', in Jane Caplan (ed.), *Nazism, Fascism and the Working Class: Essays by Tim Mason* (Cambridge: Cambridge University Press, 1995), pp. 79, 93. See also Detlev J.K. Peukert, *Inside Nazi Germany: Conformity, Opposition and Racism in Everyday Life*, trans. Richard Deveson (Harmondsworth: Penguin, 1989), p. 175. For 'society as factory', see Maier, *In Search of Stability*, ch. 1.

29 Goebbels, speech of 17 February 1939, cited in Herf, *Reactionary Modernism*, p. 196, emphasis added.

30 See Peukert, *Inside Nazi Germany*, p. 32

31 Brecht, cited in Hugh Ridley, 'Irrationalism, Art and Violence: Ernst Jünger and Gottfried Benn', in Alan Bance (ed.), *Weimar Germany: Writers and Politics* (Edinburgh: Scottish Academic Press, 1982), p. 32.

32 Jürgen Habermas, 'Modernity – an Incomplete Project', in Hal Foster (ed.), *Postmodern Culture* (London: Polity Press, 1983), p. 5.

33 Paul Fussell, *The Great War and Modern Memory* (Oxford: Oxford University Press, 1975), p. 115.

34 Roger Griffin, *The Nature of Fascism* (London: Routledge, 1993), pp. 32–6, 73–5.

35 Peter Osborne, *The Politics of Time: Modernity and Avant-Garde* (London: Verso, 1995), p. 164.

36 Tom Nairn, *The Break-up of Britain: Crisis and Neo-Nationalism*, 2nd edn (London: Verso, 1981), p. 348. See also Geoff Eley, 'What Produces Fascism: Preindustrial Traditions or a Crisis of a Capitalist State?', *Politics and Society*, vol. 12, no. 1, 1983, p. 71.

37 Bloch, *Heritage of Our Times*, p. 105.

38 See Peter Osborne, 'Times (Modern), Modernity (Conservative)? Notes on the Persistence of a Temporal Motif', *New Formations*, 28, 1996, pp. 132–41. Compare Noël O'Sullivan, *Fascism* (London: Dent, 1983), who treats fascism as non-reactionary because of its 'activist' style.

39 Theodor Adorno, *Aesthetic Theory*, trans. C. Lenhardt (London: Routledge, 1984), p. 95.

Chapter 5

1 Adolf Hitler, *Mein Kampf* (1925), trans. Ralph Manheim (Boston: Houghton Mifflin Co., 1943), p. 288.

2 Peter Staudenmaier, 'Fascist Ideology: The "Green Wing" of the Nazi Party and Its Historical Antecedents', in Janet Biehl and Peter Staudenmaier, *Ecofascism: Lessons from the German Experience* (Edinburgh: AK Press, 1995), p. 8.

3 I have adopted the title of this section from Alice Yaeger Kaplan, *Reproductions of Banality: Fascism, Literature, and French Intellectual Life* (Minneapolis: University of Minnesota Press, 1986).

4 Walther Darré, 'The Peasantry as the Key to Understanding the Nordic Race' (1929), 'Marriage Laws and the Principles of Breeding' (1930) and 'The Farmers and the State' (1931), all in Barbara Miller Lane and Leila J. Rupp, *Nazi Ideology before 1933: A Documentation* (Manchester: Manchester University Press, 1978). See also Anna Bramwell, *Blood and Soil: Walther Darré and Hitler's 'Green Party'* (Bourne End: The Kensal Press, 1985).

5 See Robert A. Pois, *National Socialism and the Religion of Nature* (London: Croom Helm, 1986), ch. 3.

6 Ibid., p. 59; Staudenmaier, 'Fascist Ideology', p. 6.

7 Cited in Staudenmaier, 'Fascist Ideology', p. 13.

8 Ernst Bloch, 'Rough Night in Town and Country' (1929), in Bloch, *Heritage of Our Times*, trans. Neville and Stephen Plaice (Cambridge: Polity, 1991).

9 Cited in Raymond H. Dominick III, 'The Nazis and the Nature Conservationists', *The Historian*, vol. 49, no. 4, 1987, p. 521. See also Dominick, *The Environmental Movement in Germany: Prophets and Pioneers, 1871–1971* (Bloomington and Indianapolis: Indianapolis University Press, 1992), Part 2.

10 See William H. Rollins, 'Whose Landscape? Technology, Fascism, and

Environmentalism on the National Socialist *Autobahn'*, *Annals of the Association of American Geographers*, vol. 85, no. 3, 1995, pp. 494–520.

11 Anna Bramwell, *Ecology in the 20th Century: A History* (New Haven, CT: Yale University Press, 1989), ch. 8.

12 Hitler, *Mein Kampf*, p. 287, emphasis added.

13 Theodor Adorno and Max Horkheimer, *Dialectic of Enlightenment*, trans. John Cumming (London: Verso, 1979), p. 27. Roland Barthes, *Mythologies*, trans. Annette Lavers (London: Paladin, 1973), pp. 142, 148–9.

14 George Mosse, *Nationalism and Sexuality: Middle-Class Morality and Sexual Norms in Modern Europe* (Madison: University of Wisconsin Press, 1985), p. 156.

15 Cited in ibid., p. 163.

16 Mussolini, cited in Henry Ashby Turner, 'Fascism and Modernization', *World Politics*, 24, 1972, p. 556. 'Every woman is by her natural destiny a mother', was how the Opera Nazionale Maternità ed Infanzia (National Agency for Maternity and Childhood) put it in 1935. See Lesley Caldwell, 'Reproducers of the Nation: Women and the Family in Fascist Policy', in David Forgacs (ed.), *Rethinking Italian Fascism: Capitalism, Populism and Culture* (London: Lawrence and Wishart, 1986), p. 141; Renate Bridenthal, Atina Grossman and Marion Kaplan (eds), *When Biology Became Destiny: Women in Weimar and Nazi Germany* (New York: Monthly Review Press, 1984).

17 The first is from the Opera Nazionale Maternità ed Infanzia, December 1934, cited in Caldwell, 'Reproducers of the Nation', p. 133; the second is from Hitler's, speech of 8 September 1934, cited in Pois, *National Socialism and the Religion of Nature*, p. 53.

18 Maria Fraddosio, 'The Fallen Hero: The Myth of Mussolini and Fascist Women in the Italian Social Republic (1943–5)', *Journal of Contemporary History*, 31, 1996, p. 108.

19 See Pois, *National Socialism and the Religion of Nature*, p. 87.

20 David Schoenbaum, *Hitler's Social Revolution: Class and Status in Nazi Germany 1933–1939* (London: Weidenfeld & Nicolson, 1967), p. 187; Tim Mason, 'Women in Germany, 1925–1940. Family, Welfare and Work', in Jane Caplan (ed.), *Nazism, Fascism and the Working Class: Essays by Tim Mason* (Cambridge: Cambridge University Press, 1995), p. 154.

21 Klaus Theweleit, *Male Fantasies, Vol. 1: Women, Floods, Bodies, History*, trans. Stephen Conway (Cambridge: Polity Press, 1987); and Theweleit *Male Fantasies, Vol. 2: Male Bodies: Psychoanalyzing the White Terror*, trans. Chris Turner and Erica Carter (Cambridge: Polity Press, 1989). Wilhelm Reich notes, in *The Mass Psychology of Fascism*, trans. Vincent R. Carfagno (Harmondsworth: Penguin, 1970), that for 'Bolshevism' in fascist texts one should read 'orgasm anxiety' (p. 161).

22 Cited in John M. Hoberman, *Sport and Political Ideology* (London:

Heinemann, 1984), p. 83, which I have relied on as a major source in the
following paragraphs.

23 Pierre Drieu La Rochelle, 'The Rebirth of European Man' (1941), in
Roger Griffin (ed.), *Fascism* (Oxford: Oxford University Press, 1995),
pp. 202–3; Robert Soucy, *Fascist Intellectual: Drieu La Rochelle*
(Berkeley: University of California Press, 1979), p. 199.

24 Cited in Hoberman, *Sport and Political Ideology*, p. 90. The combination
of bourgeois respectability and desire for the cultivation of the healthy
body served to strip nudity of its sexuality. The Nazis allowed some
former nudist journals to continue publication, but as body-building
magazines. Likewise Hans Surén's *German Gymnastics*, which went
through several editions during the Third Reich, advocated nearly
complete nudity in sports activities. But to be on public display the body
had to be carefully prepared: modelled on the Greeks – an attempt to
recapture the beautiful body of the past in the future paradise – the image
was of a hairless, smooth and bronzed body. See Mosse, *Nationalism and
Sexuality*, pp. 171–3.

25 Hoberman, *Sport and Political Ideology*, p. 79.

26 Ibid., p. 61.

27 Filippo Marinetti, 'Portrait of Mussolini' (1929), in R.W. Flint (ed.),
Selected Writings (London: Secker & Warburg, 1971), pp. 158–9. Drieu
cited in William Tucker, *The Fascist Ego: A Political Biography of Robert
Brasillach* (Berkeley: University of California Press, 1975), p. 149.

28 Ernst H. Kantorowicz, *The King's Two Bodies: A Study in Medieval
Political Theology* (Princeton, NJ: Princeton University Press, 1957).

29 Though sadly a few hangovers remain, such as the obsession with the
bodies of the Royal Family in Britain.

30 José Antonio Prima de Rivera, 'The Intellectuals and Dictatorship'
(1931), in Hugh Thomas (ed.), *José Antonio Prima de Rivera: Selected
Writings* (London: Jonathan Cape, 1972), p. 36.

31 Cited in Soucy, *Fascist Intellectual*, pp. 237–8.

32 Klaus Theweleit, *Object-Choice (All You Need is Love . . .)*, trans.
Malcolm Green (London: Verso, 1994), p. 14.

33 Space does not allow a detailed discussion of this, but for a useful account,
see Biehl and Staudenmaier, *Ecofascism*.

34 Kate Soper, *What is Nature? Culture, Politics and the Non-human*
(Oxford: Blackwell, 1995), p. 73.

35 Darré, 'Marriage Laws and the Principles of Breeding', pp. 111–12, 115.

36 That the nation is itself bisexual, as Kate Soper points out in *What is
Nature?*, p. 108, matters not in the least. The fact that the nation
combines both 'male' and 'female' qualities as 'Fatherland' and
'Motherland' does not mean that its subjects are at liberty to do the same.

37 Theweleit, *Male Fantasies, Vol. 2*, p. 13. Typical here is the fascist
opposition to homosexuality, which is thought both to deviate from
'natural' sexual behaviour and to threaten the ruling elite as a

community of men who share the key characteristics of virility and strength. Hitler's purge of the SA in 1934 – intended to placate the regular army and eliminate an organization which constituted a potential threat to his own power – enabled a purge of Ernst Röhm and other top men in the SA whose homosexuality was well established. George Mosse, *Nationalism and Sexuality*, p. 158, reports that after the purge Hitler blamed Röhm's homosexuality on his life in the tropics. Presumably, if Röhm had spent more time in German forests he would have turned out to be as normal a mass murderer as all the others.

38 Theweleit, *Male Fantasies, Vol. 2*, p. 17, building very much on Reich's account, in *The Mass Psychology of Fascism*, of the role of 'blood poisoning' in fascist ideology. J.P. Stern, *Hitler: The Führer and the People* (London: Fontana, 1984), p. 50. The parallel with recent right-wing responses to AIDS needs no comment.

39 Adorno and Horkheimer, *Dialectic of Enlightenment*, p. 234.

40 Maria-Antonietta Macciocchi, 'Female Sexuality in Fascist Ideology', *Feminist Review*, 1, 1979, p. 75.

41 In laws passed in 1933 Goering first became master of the German forests and then master of the German hunt. Hitler drily commented: 'First you protect the animals, then you shoot them dead'. Cited by Dominick, 'Nazis and the Nature Conservationists', p. 535.

42 Adorno and Horkheimer, *Dialectic of Enlightenment*, p. 235.

43 Theweleit, *Male Fantasies, Vol. 2*, p. 193. On this basis one can agree with Adorno and Horkeheimer that the desecration of cemeteries is not some kind of aberration, the work of unthinking extremists, but the very *essence* of fascism. In its obsession with death the centrality of nationalism to fascism is again apparent. As Benedict Anderson, *Imagined Communities: Reflections on the Origin and Spread of Nationalism* (London: Verso, 1991), p. 10, suggests, a good place to start an analysis of the cultural roots of *nationalism* would be with death, which lies at the heart of nationalism – witness the style and content of nationalist monuments. Can one imagine a Tomb of the Unknown Marxist or a cenotaph for fallen liberals?

Conclusion

1 John Tyndall, *The Eleventh Hour: A Call for British Rebirth* (London: Albion Press, 1988). The articulation of central fascist themes in the context of 1980s Britain produces what can only be described as some remarkable original arguments: the Conservative trade-union reforms of the early 1980s, generally held to have played a major role in curbing trade union power and thus weakening labour opposition to capital accumulation, are held by Tyndall to have been 'spineless compromises' (p. 364). One does not need to speculate too much to comprehend the

means Tyndall and other fascists in Britain would use against the working class were they to come to power.

2 See the collections in Luciano Cheles, Ronnie Ferguson and Michalina Vaughan (eds), *Neo-fascism in Europe* (London: Longman, 1991); and Paul Hainsworth (ed.), *The Extreme Right in Europe and the USA* (London: Pinter, 1992).

3 Paul Virilio, *Speed and Politics*, trans. Mark Polizzotti (New York: Semiotext(e), 1986), p. 117.

4 See Theodor Adorno, 'What Does Coming to Terms with the Past Mean?' (1959), in Geoffrey Hartman (ed.), *Bitburg in Moral and Political Perspective* (Bloomington: Indiana University Press, 1986), p. 124.

5 See Dielthem Prowe, ' "Classic" Fascism and the New Radical Right: Comparisons and Contrasts', *Contemporary European History*, vol. 3, no. 3, 1994, pp. 289–313.

6 What Andrew Gamble has rightly described as *The Free Economy and the Strong State: The Politics of Thatcherism* (London: Macmillan, 1988).

7 I have adapted this argument from Peter Osborne, 'Times (Modern), Modernity (Conservative)? Notes on the Persistence of a Temporal Motif', *New Formations*, 28, 1996, pp. 132–41.

8 Richard Thurlow, *Fascism in Britain: A History, 1918–1985* (Oxford: Blackwell, 1987), ch. 12.

9 Pierre Vidal-Naquet, *Assassins of Memory: Essays on the Denial of the Holocaust*, trans. Jeffrey Mehlman (New York: Columbia University Press, 1992), pp. 24, 98. For good accounts of the holocaust denial, see Gill Seidel, *The Holocaust Denial* (Leeds: Beyond the Pale Collective, 1986); and Roger Eatwell, 'The Holocaust Denial: A Study in Propaganda Technique', in Cheles *et al.*, *Neo-fascism in Europe*.

10 The major contributions to the debate can be found in *Forever in the Shadow of Hitler: Original Documents of the Historikerstreit, the Controversy Concerning the Singularity of the Holocaust*, trans. James Knowlton and Truett Cates (Atlantic Highlands, NJ: Humanities Press, 1993).

11 See Geoffrey Harris, *The Dark Side of Europe: The Extreme Right Today* (Edinburgh: Edinburgh University Press, 1994), p. 207. More generally, see Tobias Abse, 'Scarlet and Black: The Italian Revisionist Controversy', *Radical Philosophy*, 77, 1996, pp. 2–5.

12 'Fascist Decries Anti-Semitism', *The Guardian*, 16 September 1992.

13 See Peter Popham, 'Il Duce's Disciple', *The Independent Magazine*, 25 March 1995.

14 I have challenged the rehabilitation of Carl Schmitt in Mark Neocleous, 'Friend or Enemy? Reading Schmitt Politically', *Radical Philosophy*, 79, 1996, pp. 13–23.

Index